# EUROPEAN IMPERIALISM, 1860–1914

## Studies in European History

General Editor:    Richard Overy
Editorial Consultants:    John Breuilly
                          Roy Porter

PUBLISHED TITLES

FORTHCOMING

# EUROPEAN IMPERIALISM, 1860–1914

ANDREW PORTER

*Rhodes Professor of Imperial History, King's College*
*University of London*

First published 1994 by
MACMILLAN PRESS LTD
Houndmills, Basingstoke, Hampshire RG21 6XS
and London
Companies and representatives
throughout the world

ISBN 0-333-48104-6

A catalogue record for this book is available
from the British Library.

10   9   8   7   6   5   4   3
03   02   01   00   99   98   97

Printed in Malaysia

940·28

**Series Standing Order**

If you would like to receive future titles in this series as they are published, you can make
use of our standing order facility. To place a standing order please contact your
bookseller or, in case of difficulty,write to us at the address below with your name and
address and the name of the series. Please state with which title you wish to begin your
standing order. (If you live outside the United Kingdom we may not have the rights for
your area, in which case we will forward your order to the publisher concerned.)

Customer Services Department, Macmillan Distribution Ltd
Houndmills, Basingstoke, Hampshire RG21 6XS, England

# Contents

# A Note on References

References are cited throughout in brackets according to the numbering in the select bibliography, with page references where necessary indicated by a colon after the bibliography number.

## Acknowledgements

My thanks go to my London colleagues, in particular to Peter Marshall and Tony Stockwell (who, obliging as ever, both commented on sections of this manuscript) and Rob Holland. From all of them I have learnt much over the years, and I hope this may be of some use to their students as well as to my own.


The author and publishers are grateful for permission to use copyright material. Every effort has been made to trace all the copyright holders but if any have been inadvertently overlooked the publishers will be pleased to make the necessary arrangement at the first opportunity.

# Editor's Preface

The main purpose of this new series of studies is to make available to teacher and student alike developments in a field of history that has become increasingly specialised with the sheer volume of new research and literature now produced. These studies are designed to present the 'state of the debate' on important themes and episodes in European history since the sixteenth century, presented in a clear and critical way by someone who is closely concerned himself with the debate in question.

The studies are not intended to be read as extended bibliographical essays, though each will contain a detailed guide to further reading which will lead students and the general reader quickly to key publications. Each book carries its own interpretation and conclusions, while locating the discussion firmly in the centre of the current issues as historians see them. It is intended that the series will introduce students to historical approaches which are in some cases very new and which, in the normal course of things, would take many years to filter down into the textbooks and school histories. I hope it will demonstrate some of the excitement historians, like scientists, feel as they work away in the vanguard of their subject.

The format of the series conforms closely with that of the companion volumes of studies in economic and social history which has already established a major reputation since its inception in 1968. Both series have an important contribution to make in publicising what it is that historians are doing and in making history more open and accessible. It is vital for history to communicate if it is to survive.

R. J. OVERY

vii

# A Chronology of Events

1858     June: Treaties of Tientsin between China and Britain, France, USA, and Russia; Russo-Chinese treaty cedes control of Amur region to Russia. French occupation of Saigon.

1860     October: Peking Conventions signed with Britain and France.

1861     August: British annexation of Lagos.

1862     June: Treaty of Saigon, recognises French protectorate over three eastern provinces of Cochin-China. British representative established at Mandalay.

1863     August: French protectorate over Cambodia. International settlement founded at Shanghai. Dutch complete annexation of Borneo.

1864     France annexes Loyalty Islands.

1865     Russia captures Tashkent.

1866–76     Russia subdues Central Asian khanates of Kokand, Khiva and Bokhara.

1867     France annexes western provinces of Cochin-China; declares protectorate over Rapa. USA acquires Midway Is.

1868     Britain's Abyssinian Expedition. August: French Treaty of Commerce and Friendship with Hova rulers of Madagascar.

1869     November: Suez Canal opened.

1870     June: massacre of foreigners in Tientsin. July: outbreak of Franco-Prussian war.

1871     Japan claims sovereignty over Ryuku Islands. Anglo-Dutch Treaty of Sumatra. Spanish conquest of Sulu (1871–8). October: Britain annexes Griqualand West.

| 1873–4 | Japan considers occupation of Formosa; French intervention at Hanoi (Garnier Affair); Second Anglo-Ashanti War; beginnings of Dutch war with Acheh (1873–1903). |
|---|---|
| 1874 | March: Annam a French protectorate, and Cochin-China a French colony; June: British Treaty of Pangkor, with Perak rulers, and Perak, Selangor and Sungei Ujong brought under control; October: Britain annexes Fiji. |
| 1875 | November: Britain purchases Suez Canal shares from the Khedive of Egypt. |
| 1876 | Anglo-Chinese Chefoo Convention; Germany annexes bases in Marshall Islands (1876, 1878); September: International Geographical Conference in Brussels, convened by Leopold II of the Belgians, who forms the International African Association. |
| 1877 | April: British annexation of South African Republic (Transvaal). Russo-Turkish War (April 1877–March 1878). |
| 1878 | March: Russo-Turkish Treaty of San Stefano; June–July: Congress of Berlin, and British occupation of Cyprus. Leopold II establishes Comité d'études du Haut Congo. March: British protectorate over Walvis Bay, South-West Africa. Anglo-German-USA treaties recognise independence of Samoa (1878–9), and USA secures use of Pago Pago harbour. Second Anglo-Afghan War (1878–9). |
| 1879 | January–September: Anglo-Zulu War. May: Treaty of Gandamak between Britain and Afghanistan. September: Anglo-French Dual Control of Egyptian finances confirmed. |
| 1880 | Tahiti a French colony, and French protectorates over Raiatea and Leeward Islands. July: international Madrid Convention recognises independence and integrity of Morocco. First Anglo-Boer War (December 1880–March 1881). |
| 1881 | Charter granted to British North Borneo Company. April–May: French occupation of Tunis followed by Treaty of Bardo, establishing French protectorate. |

| | |
|---|---|
| 1882 | July–September: British occupation of Egypt; November: French approval of S. de Brazza's Congo treaties; December: British recognition of Portuguese claims to the Congo. Italian occupation of Assab. |
| 1883 | August: Treaty of Hue results in French protectorate over Annam. December: French occupy Tonkin, and Sino-French war begins. German New Guinea Company granted a charter. |
| 1884 | February: Anglo-Portuguese Congo Treaty; April, July: German protectorates at Angra Pequena, Togoland and Cameroons. Britain and France establish Somali protectorates. British and German annexations of New Guinea. Berlin West Africa Conference (November 1884–February 1885). French occupation of Cambodia. |
| 1885 | January: Spanish protectorate over Rio de Oro and Spanish Guinea; General Gordon killed at Khartoum, and Anglo-Egyptian forces withdraw from the Sudan. February: the Berlin Act, includes recognition of the Congo Free State; German East Africa protectorate established, and Italy occupies Massawa. April: Anglo-Russian Penjdeh (Afghanistan) crisis begins. June: British Niger Coast Protectorate; Sino-French Treaty of Tientsin recognises French domination of Indo-China. October–November: Third Anglo-Burmese War. December: French protectorate over Madagascar finally established. |
| 1886 | January: Britain annexes Upper Burma. July: Britain's Royal Niger Company receives charter. October–November: Anglo-German Agreement on East Africa. Witwatersrand (South Africa) goldfields opened. |
| 1887 | January: Italo-Abyssinian war begins (1887–9). December: Portugal secures Macao. Informal Anglo-Russian division of Persia into spheres of interest. France unites Cochin-China, Annam, Cambodia and Tonkin in the Union Indo-Chinoise. Anglo-French Pacific condominium over New Hebrides. |

| 1888 | March, May: British protectorates over Sarawak, Brunei and N.Borneo. September: charter granted to the Imperial British East Africa Company. British protectorate over Cook Islands. |
|------|------|
| 1889 | August: Anglo-French agreement on Gold and Ivory Coasts, Senegal and Gambia. October: charter granted to British South Africa Company. |
| 1890 | French war with Dahomey, ends in recognition of protectorate. July: international Brussels Act, concerning the slave trade; Anglo-German agreement resolves East African disputes over Zanzibar and Tanganyika. August: Anglo-French agreement defines their Niger territories. |
| 1891 | March–April: Anglo-Italian Red Sea agreements. June: Anglo-Dutch treaty defines their Borneo territories; Anglo-Portuguese agreement over East and Central Africa. July: Portugal grants charters to Mozambique and Niassa Companies. |
| 1892 | British protectorate over Gilbert and Ellice Islands. |
| 1893 | February: Nyasaland becomes British Central African Protectorate. British South Africa Company war against the Ndebele. France acquires protectorate over Laos. |
| 1894 | August: outbreak of Sino-Japanese war over Korea. November: French begin conquest of Madagascar. |
| 1895 | March: Italian advance into Abyssinia. April: Treaty of Shimonoseki, by which China recognises Korean independence and cedes other territory to Japan, with important consequences for their relations with the major European powers. July: following collapse of Imperial British East Africa Company, Britain establishes the East Africa Protectorate. Anglo-American dispute over Venezuela boundary. Anglo-Transvaal relations deteriorate. Fourth Anglo-Ashanti War (1895–August 1896). |
| 1896 | January: failure of Dr Jameson's Raid into the Transvaal; Anglo-French agreement guarantees independence of Siam, and recognises French position in Laos. March: Italians defeated at Adowa by Abyssinia. June: Sino-Russian Treaty. July: British |

|      | federation of Malay States (Perak, Selangor, Negri Sembilan, Pahang). Britain begins reconquest of the Sudan. |
|------|---|
| 1897 | June: USA treaty of annexation with Hawaii. November: Germany seizes Kiaowchow, precipitating a European scramble for concessions in China (1897–9). |
| 1898 | January: Russian occupation of Port Arthur. April–December: Spanish American War, with USA acquiring the Philippines, Puerto Rico and Guam. June: Anglo-French boundary agreement ends crisis over Niger territories; Britain leases Kowloon and Weihaiwei. August: Anglo-German agreement on future of Portuguese colonies. September: British victory at Omdurman, completes reconquest of Sudan and paves way for Anglo-Egyptian condominium. September–November: the Anglo-French Fashoda Crisis. |
| 1899 | March: Anglo-French convention resolves disputes over the Sudan. Germany acquires Mariana and Caroline (Palau) Islands. Boxer Rising begins in China. October: outbreak of South African War between Britain and Transvaal. November: Baghdad railway concession granted to German syndicate. December: Britain, Germany and USA divide the protectorate of Samoa, followed by Britain's acquisition of Solomon Islands and Tonga. |
| 1900 | The Boxer War in China. December: Franco-Italian agreement recognises claims respectively in Morocco and Tripoli. |
| 1902 | January: Anglo-Japanese alliance. May: the South African War ends with Treaty of Vereeniging. |
| 1904 | January: outbreak of Herero revolt in German South-West Africa (1904–7). February: outbreak of Russo-Japanese War. April: Anglo-French entente recognises respective interests in Egypt and Morocco, and settles all outstanding colonial disputes. |
| 1905 | March–April: first Franco-German Moroccan crisis. September: Russo-Japanese peace treaty signed at |

Portsmouth, settles position of Korea, Sakhalin and Manchuria.

1906  January: international Algeciras Conference on future of Morocco. July: Tripartite Pact between Britain, France and Italy, agreeing status of Abyssinia.

1907  March–April: Siamese independence confirmed by Britain and France. August: Anglo-Russian entente, includes agreements over Tibet, Afghanistan and Persia.

1908  Bali under Dutch rule. October: Belgium assumes direct control of Congo State from Leopold II.

1909  February: Franco-German agreement over Morocco. March: Anglo-Siamese treaty places Unfederated Malay States (Kelantan, Trengganu, Kedah, Perlis) under British protection, subsequently endorsed by local agreements. Formation of the Anglo-Persian Oil Company.

1910  August: Japan annexes Korea.

1911  July–November: second Franco-German Moroccan (Agadir) crisis. October: outbreak of the Chinese Revolution. November: Italy, at war with Turkey since September, annexes Tripoli and Cyrenaica.

1912  March: Treaty of Fez establishes French protectorate over Morocco. The Chinese Republic established.

# 1  Definitions and Theories

'Imperialism' has always been a diffuse and emotive subject, even when there is broad agreement on what is being considered. Recent writings have done little to dispel this problem, and any discussion almost immediately exposes a semantic minefield. Words like 'political', 'social', 'cultural' or 'economic' are unavoidable, but, ordinary though they may be, they are difficult to use precisely; the boundaries between the things they describe are rarely clear-cut. Of course, all historians face this problem. Although many solve it to their own satisfaction by labelling themselves 'political' or 'economic' historians, historians of imperialism cannot specialise in quite the same way. The interest of the subject, as well as its frustrations, lies in the fact that it embraces all these subdivisions. Its study involves historians in attempting both to define and disentangle a wide range of social, political or economic processes, in order to understand their distinct function and perhaps their importance relative to each other. These tasks of identification, disentanglement and assessment are unavoidably contentious. Even the title of this essay will raise the hackles of at least some readers! However, the problem of definition seems as appropriate a spot as any at which to start.

Territorial empires are familiar, historically speaking, found at all periods and in all shapes and sizes. They are associated with cities (Rome, Venice), dynasties (the Carolingians or the Hapsburgs), individuals (Napoleon I, Hitler), and, above all, with particular countries or states (Spain, Holland, Britain, Russia). This essay, however, is not primarily concerned with detailed study of either one such empire or several. Nor does it focus, except indirectly, on the phenomenon of 'colonial-

1

ism', whether understood as the manner in which imperial powers have run colonies and other parts of their empires – in other words, the patterns of colonial rule – or as the condition of subject peoples. Again, it does not enter into the extensive debates about the objective long-term consequences of imperial domination, either for subordinate territories in the shapes of 'neo-colonialism', 'under-development', 'dependency' and 'modernisation', or for the imperial powers themselves.

Its subject is imperialism considered as the processes by which either formal empires or significant influence and control short of direct rule – 'informal' empires – came into being and then grew. It looks at the dynamics of modern empire-building and forms of domination or coercion employed as part of those processes. Its purpose is to offer some guidance into the vast literature, and in particular to sketch out the main areas and issues of current interest to historians. Chronologically it confines itself to the period 1860–1914, often referred to as that of the 'New Imperialism', when exclusive claims to territory by European powers and their attempts to assert effective control, as well as other forms of European intervention and influence overseas, proliferated more quickly than they had done since the eighteenth century and attracted an unusual degree of attention.

Both subject and period are thus somewhat strictly defined. This is for reasons other than that of limited space. The century from 1815–1914 is recognised as one in which the mutual awareness, interconnection and interdependence of most parts of the world, which had developed since the early sixteenth century, grew at a startling rate and reached unprecedented levels. This growth of an integrated world had different facets, many of them linked to the growth in size and complexity of an international or world economy [277; 300]. A huge expansion of world trade occurred, made possible in particular by the growth of global telegraph, railway and shipping networks, cheaper transport and lower marketing costs. The rise in overseas capital investments and large-scale migration, especially of Europeans, Indians and Chinese, contributed to this increase. Economic exchanges and technological advance, however, were only part of the picture. There developed new global rivalries and ambitions to dominate or rule overseas territories, involving Japan and the United States of America as well as the major European countries, together with the extended military and naval defence systems required for states' self-protection. The spread of knowledge of the 'outside world' was also remarkable, especially but not only in Europe with its high levels of literacy. With powerful motive impulses coming from the Atlantic or European world, these broad processes of global integration and European expansion are commonly but loosely linked together as the characteristics of an age of 'imperialism' shaped by the technologically advanced capitalist societies of the west.

Within this general picture of increasing interdependence between different regions of the world, there occurred more specific forms of 'imperialism', perceived by all parties as involving varying degrees of subordination and control by European powers [1–38; 316; 320]. These different phenomena, of expansion and imperialism, are frequently confused with each other, being difficult to separate even when no more than tangentially connected. There is therefore value in selecting a period in which European expansion broadly conceived coincided with numerous instances of a more narrowly defined, often territorial 'imperialism', so that one might try not only to examine the latter but to place them in a wider setting. The early 1860s mark the point at which a temporary political and economic equilibrium in Europe began to break down, ushering in just such a period.

Quite clearly between 1860 and 1914 a very wide range of forms of empire-building was in operation. Historians are confronted with both a multiplicity of instances of imperialism, however defined, and a number of states and empires in the throes of expansion. 'Imperialism' was so widespread both in terms of the involvement of European states and the extent of its world-wide development, that if a more general unity existed which in fact encompassed or underpinned particular national empires, then it is likely to be revealed by study of this period if any [299].

A brief outline of European states' mounting formal expansion abroad usefully illustrates the scale of the phenomenon we are concerned with. Although several European states were already by 1860 'imperial' powers in the formal sense of possessing overseas colonies, this did not normally inhibit their further expansion. Most striking was Great Britain, which already directly ruled or dominated the greater part of India, had several footholds in West Africa (notably in the Gambia and Sierra Leone) and larger southern holdings in the Cape Colony and Natal, Asian staging posts in Penang, Singapore and Hong Kong, and held in their entirety Australia, New Zealand and Canada. Notwithstanding these and other responsibilities such as her Caribbean possessions, Britain acquired very large areas of Africa in all regions south of the Sahara. She became the *de facto* ruler of Egypt; established spheres of influence, varying in intensity, in the Arabian peninsula, in Persia, and in southern China focused on the Yangtze valley; and extended her power in Burma, much of the Malay peninsula, more of Borneo, and into the Pacific [10–13; 298].

The British record was paralleled by that of France, particularly in Africa. Earlier conquests in Algeria were extended south and west into Morocco, while those in Senegal were pushed inland, with the result that much of the Sahara and Western Sudan fell to France. Dahomey, the Ivory Coast, Gabon, French Equatorial Africa, parts of both the Congo and Somaliland, together with Tunisia and Madagascar followed. Indo-China was conquered, and French spheres of influence were established in China and, more firmly, the Pacific [14–17; 220]. The Portuguese, although unable to build on the fag-ends of their former empire which were scattered from Macao, Timor and Goa in Asia to Sao Tomé and Guinea Bissau in West Africa, nevertheless fought vigorously to extend and give reality to their historic holdings in Angola and Mozambique [25; 26; 33]. Russia's longstanding expansion to the south and east continued. Central Asia was subjugated by 1895; a sphere of influence was formally established in northern Persia; the Amur District and the island of Sakhalin were acquired; and Manchuria was occupied for a few years until 1905, after which Russia retained a sphere of influence in the north under her 1907 agreement with Japan [27–29; 304; 313].

Other newly established states and individuals entered the

colonial fray for the first time, again taking particular advantage of the general partition of African territory. In 1884–90 Germany staked her claims to South-West Africa (Namibia), Tanganyika, Togo and Kamerun; elsewhere she acquired Samoa, a Pacific sphere including the Marshall and Caroline Islands and part of New Guinea, and a sphere of influence in Shantung (northern China) [18; 19; 164; 168; 175; 301; 302; 306; 314]. Italy gained Tripoli, parts of Somaliland and Eritrea, and was only prevented by military defeat at Adowa in 1896 from grasping Ethiopia (Abyssinia). Her ambitions too reached the Far East, resulting in the lease of Ningpo [20]. King Leopold II of the Belgians, after coveting various parts of the globe, finally acquired in central Africa the gigantic Congo Free State [9; 301].

If the Scandinavians harboured imperial ambitions they kept them to themselves, and the Danes abandoned their remaining West African trading forts in 1850. Of the older colonial powers, the Dutch too shared the new expansionist enthusiasms. Although they too got out of Africa in 1872, they thereafter concentrated on the 'thirty years war' of subjugation in Acheh (1873–1903) and the piecemeal but steady extension and development of their other long-held possessions in the East Indies (especially Java and Borneo) [21–24]. Although Russia sold Alaska in 1867, only Spain actually lost colonies, by conquest rather than carelessness, when Cuba and the Philippines passed to the USA and Pacific claims to Germany, after the Spanish-American War of 1898. Some recompense was found, however, in the shape of new Spanish gains in Africa – the Rio De Oro, Spanish Sahara and Rio Muni [30–33].

Despite the literature and debate generated especially since 1960 by study of this global transformation, newly published work continues to provoke lively argument and further research. Even in outline, the scale and complexity of European empire-building in this period provide indications of the intrinsic interest and historical importance of the subject, as well as a sufficient justification for historians' continued preoccupation with it. In addition this preoccupation arises from more contemporary concerns. Recently historians have devoted serious attention to the collapse and disappearance of European colonial empires, in that further global readjustment involved since 1945 in the process of 'decolonisation' [34–38]. There is no doubt that our understanding of imperial decline or decolonisation, of 'the end of empire', will be influenced in many ways by our interpretation of the earlier phases of expansion [313]. Furthermore, 'imperialism' is not only recognised by historians as a perennial and recurrent phenomenon. The word itself has long since passed into the language of contemporary politics. Not only are many states conscious of living with the legacy of empires past; along with political commentators and analysts of every kind, they are on the watch for imperial ambition in the present. Iranians, for example, feel that they know 'the Great Satan' – the USA – only too well, while Israel and Iraq are both widely feared by their neighbours. This results in the drawing of analogies, for instance, between recent United States policy and that of European powers in their expansionist heyday [6; 8]. The quality of contemporary discussion of international affairs depends on the accuracy of such analogies, and those in turn are reliant consciously or unconsciously on the understanding we may have of Europe's own past.

Nevertheless, it can be plausibly argued that continuing debate creates more heat than light, especially in the absence of agreement about the very meaning of the word 'imperialism'. Keith Hancock is remembered not only as a distinguished and versatile historian but for the dictum that imperialism is 'no word for scholars'. He was not alone in thinking that its imprecision makes it descriptively and analytically useless. Its semantic history, for example, reveals a process of constant redefinition, from an original specific application to policies of Napoleon III to the development of negative as well as positive connotations as its relationship with 'capitalism' came under scrutiny at the beginning of this century [43; 44; 51; 52]. The types of influence or control embraced by the word have steadily increased to include 'capitalist', 'commercial', 'cultural', 'financial' and 'business' imperialism, 'the imperialism of free trade' and the 'subimperialisms' of client states, 'military', 'jurisdictional', 'ecological', 'railway' and 'missionary' imperialism, 'social' imperialism and the imperialism of technology [e.g. 230; 234; 297].

6

In particular, this proliferation of imperialisms was encouraged by the argument that historians should recognise the existence of 'informal' empire. This term has been applied to those situations in which one power's domination or significant control of another's local affairs existed outside any formalised political framework of imperial rule. Informal empire followed perhaps as a matter of course from the commercial links between the states concerned, and was likely to be kept in place with occasional demonstrations of force or other forms of pressure by the 'imperial' partner. The further idea, that imperial powers or their agents might choose to employ and develop the techniques of either informal control or formal rule as circumstances required, has prompted much argument about the continuity or discontinuity of 'imperialism' throughout the nineteenth century and beyond. Disputes have focused, first, on the problem of drawing the line between 'formal' and 'informal' categories. They have also arisen from the suggestion that the 'New Imperialism' is a mirage, and that in the case, for example, of Britain during the nineteenth century, no significant break in approaches to empire can be established [10; 46; 50; 54; 237].

The problem has also been compounded by suggestions that our understanding of European imperialism should not be confined to relations between metropolitan states and extra-European areas. The concept of 'internal colonialism' attempts to pinpoint the process of imperialism within Europe, by examining those weaker less-developed areas in some way dominated by or tributary to other stronger and more prosperous centres. These might involve regions within states such as Brittany and the Massif Central, Wales or southern Italy; or it might cover states such as those in the Balkans or Portugal, seen as peripheral within Europe but at least vulnerable to pressure if not tied by trade or finance to others more powerful, such as Austria, Turkey, Britain or France [47; 59]. With the dissolution of chronological and spatial limits to analysis of 'imperialism', and when almost every kind of human activity or exchange may apparently contribute to the process of empire-building or the establishment of dominant influences in other countries, 'imperialism' can indeed seem virtually redundant.

Careful definitions of important terms and descriptions of events associated with them, of course, provide ways of coping with disorderly evidence and varied usage; they can focus discussion and at least temporarily inhibit further random mutations. They are a necessary accompaniment to explanation and the development of theories of empire. Study of late nineteenth-century European imperialism has spawned many such attempts at systematisation, most of which have addressed 'imperialism' in the broadest sense of world-wide economic expansion and intensified international rivalry. Some of these are worth recalling either because they have provided useful reference points to which later historians have frequently returned, or for the illustrations they offer of the difficulty in devising any descriptively or analytically effective definition.

In the early years of this century, writers such as J.A. Hobson, Joseph Schumpeter and Lenin not only attempted to define and account for 'imperialism' on the evidence of global developments between 1860 and 1918, but were contemporaries with the events they tried to analyse. How seriously one takes them may depend on one's views about the drawbacks of any contemporary analysis; on one's sense of their individual reliance on faith, *a priori* theorising and impressionistic judgement rather than on critical research and detailed knowledge; and on whether one thinks they wished to explain the past, the present or the future. The relevance of their ideas to more specific manifestations of imperial dynamism is also often doubtful. However, their influence on subsequent understanding has been huge [40; 48; 53; 55; 58].

In discussions of imperialism, there has been constant confusion between initial hypotheses as to how 'the facts' might be explained, theories which after careful investigation explained those and other 'facts', and definitions drawing together the principal characteristics of 'the facts'. This is unsurprising, given that even the factual basis of what might constitute imperialism has been uncertain. Within the Marxist tradition, Lenin's famous formulation provides a perfect illustration.

Imperialism is capitalism in that stage of development in which the domination of monopolies and finance capital

8

has taken shape; in which the export of capital has acquired pronounced importance; in which the division of the world by the international trusts has begun, and in which the partition of all the territory of the earth by the greatest capitalist countries has been completed. [53:*81*]

It appeared to be definitive, was in fact essentially hypothetical, but nevertheless claimed to provide a general theory. Since the phenomenon which it purported to explain was also unclear, it was long understood to be directed to the expansion of colonial empires between 1860 and 1910, when in fact Lenin, writing in 1915/16, intended to explain the international circumstances of the First World War and the future of capitalism [60].

Other influential writers in this first analytical phase adopted very different approaches. Unlike Lenin, Hobson regarded capitalism as fundamentally beneficial and progressive for all. Working particularly from his knowledge of South Africa and the Far East, he argued that imperialism involved the aggressive search for, and international conflict over, territory or spheres of influence providing markets and outlets for investment; it represented the perversion of true capitalism by a minority of business elites and vested interests for their own selfish purposes, through the exercise of illegitimate and undemocratic influence over governments and mass opinion [56; 258].

Schumpeter, sharing Hobson's view of capitalism as benign and focusing on the same aggressiveness in international affairs, defined imperialism as 'the objectless disposition on the part of a state to unlimited forcible expansion'. He differed from Hobson in attributing such a disposition not to the work of minority capitalist interests who might gain from it, but to the continuing influence in government and society of older, pre-capitalist social groups swayed by autocratic, militaristic values [44; 58]. Our attention has also been drawn recently to the existence before 1914 of a rather different set of theories, those providing systematic economic justifications for the necessary adoption of imperialist programmes by states in their international dealings [43; 44].

It is now possible to have a much better understanding of

these early analyses, their subsequent development, limits and later accretions, thanks not least to excellent critical surveys of the theoretical literature by Anthony Brewer, Norman Etherington and others [40; 44; 313: *Pt.4*; 317]. Historians have become increasingly sensitive to the varied meanings attached to the word 'theory', the distinct and limited purposes which individual theories could serve, and the extent to which the empirical content of theoretical formulae differed according to a writer's position. In particular, they now insist on drawing clear distinctions between (i) the expansion of capitalism, which as a type of economic activity could assume several forms; (ii) the emergence, under various conditions either associated with that expansion or largely separate from it, of elements of domination or control in relations between different societies, which might be identified as instances of informal imperialism; and (iii) the expansion of formal colonial holdings, characteristic of some but certainly not all capitalist societies. The necessity to take into account local conditions in the non-European society as well as the European is also recognised as inescapable.

The consequence of all this has been to induce in many people a wariness of definitions or general explanatory theories. Many recent definitions display a notably greater caution and striving for neutrality. There are the very general, where imperialism is, for example, 'the tendency of one society or state to control another, by whatever means and for whatever purpose' [45: *1*]. Using the example of nineteenth-century Britain it has been suggested that: 'Imperialism, perhaps, may be defined as a sufficient political function of [the] process of integrating new regions into the expanding economy' [46: *5*]. With reference to a particular period of expanding empires like 1860–1914, and involving a similar genuflection towards the importance of wilful decision, we have 'the deliberate act or advocacy of extending or maintaining a state's direct or indirect political control over any inhabited territory', and 'effective long-term political and territorial domination of the technologically superior nations over technologically inferior nations as colonies and semi-colonies' [39: *8*; 45: *3–4*]. If these are felt to blur distinctions required between types of empire, the intensification of formal colonial

10

control, and imperialism, then the latter might be pinpointed as 'the acquisition by various means of a predominant influence or direct control over the political and/or economic development of weaker, less technologically advanced peoples or states'.

Although these definitions seem unemotive and helpful only in the sense of keeping looser and utterly uncritical usage at bay, that may be the most we can hope for [57]. Given the common deployment of 'imperialism' and its derivatives for purposes of political abuse, it would perhaps also be no mean achievement. There is nevertheless still disagreement as to whether it is possible, even necessary, for a single definition or theory to cover either all these things or still more, such as the main effects of imperialism and colonialism and the possibilities of their abolition and transformation. Marxist theorists naturally reject any theory which fails to link the generation of imperialism closely to fundamental requirements of capitalism. Moreover, pursuit of theory is neither solely a Marxist nor an exclusively European activity. Although many non-European writers have taken over and added to Marxist perspectives, in the writings of others notable differences of approach and emphasis from those of the writers mentioned so far are clearly to be seen. These include a concern with the violence and barbarity of the process by which European conquest often destroyed existing societies regardless of their viability and capacity for change [49].

The search for a general theory consequently goes on, partly because, in the absence of any widespread agreement and faced with the findings of new scholarship, it seems to some historians not just an intellectual challenge but a professional obligation [55: *149*]. Brewer clearly believes that imperialism can be embraced comfortably within 'a coherent theory of the evolution of capitalism on a world scale', while accepting that 'such a theory has yet to be worked out in detail' [40: *23–4*] Benjamin Cohen speaks not least for many political scientists in arguing that 'the real taproot of imperialism – [is] the anarchic organization of the international system of states', itself rooted in turn in the persistence of national differences and hence in human nature [41: *245*].

Somewhat more sophisticated and firmly rooted in historical detail is Doyle's social-scientific work on empires [42]. Experimenting with a definition of empire as 'foreign political control over effective sovereignty' which he admits is ambiguous, he examines with particular reference to late nineteenth-century Africa some of the many combinations of influences – the processes of imperialism – which brought about that control. He distinguishes imperial power from different conditions, for example suzerainty, with reference to its scope or domain, weight and duration. 'Empire then is a relationship, formal or informal, in which one state controls the effective political sovereignty of another political society. It can be achieved by force, by political collaboration, by economic, social, or cultural dependence. Imperialism is simply the process or policy of establishing and maintaining an empire.'

Definition, however, does not lead him to a general theory. Instead, the complex nature of imperialism, he concludes, is amenable less to the application of theory than to detailed historical analysis, which is required for three purposes: to 'demonstrate the existence of control', 'explain why one party expands and establishes such control', and 'explain why the other party submits or fails to resist effectively' [42: 45–6]. General theories have been relatively simple to construct, and consequently inadequate, because they have normally rested on no more than a partial percentage of these purposes. Moreover, they have often neglected the need to integrate the domestic, colonial and international components of European states' experience. Theories are frequently, therefore, of less help in advancing our knowledge or understanding, and less capable of comprehending the realities of European imperialism, than careful historical explanation. However, Doyle is inclined to overlook the fact that even the most elementary narrative has theoretical implications: it rests on assumptions as to what requires explanation and is pertinent evidence. Historians therefore need constantly to remember the limitations of their art.

In a world where definitions and theoretical models of imperialism vary so considerably it is nevertheless essential to remind ourselves that possibilities of agreement do still exist. There is little dispute about either the existence of empires *per se*, or a wide range of processes, conscious and unconscious, involved in their construction. At the heart of debate there are also a number of common concerns: (i) to determine the actual extent of particular types of empire; (ii) to establish both which processes were the most important in their creation, and the priority to be attached at different times to each of these processes in individual cases of empire-building; (iii) to understand the extent to which individual empires or instances of imperialism may be part of a wider phenomenon.

# 2  'Metropolitan' Explanations: Political

Many explanations of imperialism have attached special importance to one central causal factor. There has been a long tradition of treating European imperialism as the direct offspring of the continent's political, essentially diplomatic, calculations. This is justified in one very obvious sense. Foreign policy-makers, both ministers and their officials, were immediately responsible for the international negotiations inseparable from the initial statement and ultimate confirmation of claims to territory; they also presided over the recognition of spheres of influence, delimitation of boundaries, and agreements over trade, concessions or international loans, as well as the definition of different nationals' rights. 'Diplomatic' interpretations, however, have deeper roots in examinations of European states' foreign policy as a whole. From this angle, non-European issues in our period only loomed really large between c. 1880 and c. 1912; even then they were rarely seen as vitally important in their own right, being treated as means to more important European ends (which is why, for example, the Fashoda Crisis of 1898 did not result in an Anglo-French war): and ultimately they contributed only secondarily to the fundamental antagonisms which brought European war in 1914.

It has often been argued that the diplomats' first object was to safeguard a balance of power in Europe favourable to their own country. Because the existing balance was both upset by the emergence of a unified Germany and French defeat in 1870, and incapable of rectification inside Europe short of renewed war, claims were made to territory and influence overseas. As the British Foreign Secretary, George Canning, had claimed in 1826, new worlds were being called in to

14

redress the imbalance of the old. Such views owe much to studies of Bismarck's diplomacy in the 1880s. Emphasis is placed on Germany's encouragement of French ambitions in Tunisia, on her exploitation of Egyptian issues in order to win French gratitude and prevent her rapprochement with Britain; Bismarck's colonial initiatives and Mediterranean diplomacy are presented as establishing a German pattern of overseas interventions, designed to demonstrate to Britain the perils of isolation and the desirability of closer relations with the Reich [93; 128; 131]. Britain too encouraged colonial ambitions in others for her own European ends, most notably perhaps in the case of Italy's designs on Tripoli and Somaliland, but also elsewhere in hopes of retaining a measure of French goodwill as Franco-Russian relations blossomed in the early 1890s [99; 107].

'Diplomatic' explanations have tended in effect to minimise the significance of imperialism for Europe's states, by treating issues of territory, dominant influence and control overseas as generally of limited importance even to a very restricted professional elite. This approach to imperial issues thus holds out the possibility of cutting students of imperialism and their subject down to size, by insisting that they recognise the limitations of their enquiries, and cultivate instead a better sense of proportion when considering what were the dominant interests of European states and the priorities of their governing classes. There is some value in this. An essential step on the road to comprehending 'imperialism' is to recognise that no more than most other issues was overseas expansion a full-time preoccupation for contemporaries. Arguments about specialists' blinkered vision, however, can be dangerously double-edged, in this case courting the response that diplomatic historians are no less prone than others to exaggerate the importance of their field.

Although older studies of Europe's late nineteenth-century diplomacy were by no means always narrowly conceived [96; 97], scholars have of late become much more aware of the dangers of discussing not just the diplomacy of imperialism but any diplomacy as if the archives of the different foreign offices contain all we need to know in order to understand it. Those who might once have billed themselves as 'diplomatic historians' increasingly recognise the need to have a much broader understanding, both of the context in which conflicting imperialisms were handled and of the wide range of preoccupations which could influence politicians in the making of foreign policy. This is seen, for example, in the following observation:

> In its most general sense, imperialism before 1914 refers to the direct (or formal) and indirect (or informal) rule which the developed, capitalist, industrial states exercised over the less developed regions and peoples. This minimal consensus requires that we explain the political, socio-economic and psychological causes and conditions that prompted the imperialism of the 'metropole'. [27:2]

Foreign policy-makers have never operated in a vacuum, and it is essential to ask detailed questions in order to elicit the full range of considerations which they derived from their wider perceptions of the world about them and consequently brought to bear on their diplomacy [94; 116].

In the light of recent work on Germany in this period, considered below, it is extremely difficult to regard many previous studies of Bismarck's diplomacy on colonial questions and empire-building as other than partial and old-fashioned, despite their insights and technical skill [79; 80; 126; 133–135]. Following recent German leads and the pressure for broader approaches, it has been suggested, for example, that the roots of Disraeli's and Gladstone's imperialism may lie both earlier and deeper than has often been thought. In both cases explanations based on a traditional concern with balance of power politics, or on the desire to adopt a striking foreign policy for party-political purposes, have been presented as at best a small part of the story [84; 85; 127]. The interplay between Lord Salisbury's conservatism in domestic or financial matters and his handling of foreign affairs has also attracted new attention. This work highlighted his anxiety to avoid the damaging impact on the landed classes of taxes to pay for increased defence spending, and thus suggests additional reasons for the restraint and caution which became so characteristic of his handling of imperial questions

[114]. The confusion and bungling of French diplomacy revealed by studies on the origins of the Fashoda debacle again illustrate the importance of looking increasingly widely for the determinants of the diplomacy of imperialism [61; 62].

What has happened over the last twenty years or so is a pronounced shift away from a primary concern with diplomatic manoeuvres and the details of the exchanges themselves. More attention is being paid instead to wider questions: why and by whom were certain overseas matters thought important in the first place? What dictated decisions to persist with selected issues, and why were certain approaches to negotiation or particular outcomes preferred over others? It may be objected that the best practitioners of diplomatic history have never ignored these considerations. To such careful scrutiny, however, has been added a marked reluctance to assume that diplomatic priorities are essentially self-evident or speak largely for themselves in the despatches of Foreign Offices. Few would now accept that Bismarck was thinking only, or even primarily, of the balance of power as affected by territorial exchange and acquisition when he told Eugen Wolf in 1888 that his own map of Africa lay in Europe [69; 110; 126].

Historians have developed a sense that foreign policy-makers were less than the free agents they have often been made to seem. As a result it is now possible to argue that diplomatic initiatives were commonly of only indirect or subordinate importance in the process of empire-building. The diplomacy of imperialism ought rather to be regarded as one of the means by which more basic demands or pressures were mediated and sometimes transformed into the substance of empire. Even where, as with Bismarck or Jules Ferry, concern with a continental balance of power was undoubtedly an important part of statesmen's calculations, the issue cannot rest there. The phrase 'balance of power' itself is notoriously ambiguous. One must also ask in what sense did imperial influence or possessions carry weight in the balance of power? Did their impact upon it lie in their mere existence, in their symbolic importance? Or did they make a material contribution to the resources of the imperial powers? In what way was India a real source of Britain's strength, or Central and East

17

Asian territories more than a drain on Russia's limited resources? These are questions to which we shall return below.

In considering further the metropolitan 'political' springs of imperialism, one must look at the powerful preoccupation of many people with national prestige. By emphasising the 'prestige' factor, states' standing in the eyes of European rivals and extra-European peoples, diplomatic historians also first began to broaden their outlook and to place the diplomacy of imperialism within its political and social context. The example of France is especially important here. Not only did the French share the common preoccupation with enhancing national standing both for reasons of self-esteem and in the eyes of others, but they interpreted it above all in terms of influence and possessions abroad. The reasons for this were various, but included an imperial past, pride in the revolutionary and Napoleonic legacies, and republican search for 'respectability'. Above all, defeat by Germany in 1870 necessitated redress and compensation: since this was impossible in Europe at least for the time being, an expansionist approach to opportunities overseas offered (as it had done before in France's history) an obvious if partial solution. An interpretation of French imperialism after 1870 within this general framework is now well established [15;16].

This is not to say that all colonial incidents or imperial issues excited nationalist sentiments; far from it. The Third Republic's enthusiasm for empire-building, at least by the state and at public expense, was at best fitful; a sense of national grievance was perfectly compatible with widespread indifference or hostility to imperial expansion [61; 62; 92]. Nevertheless, there developed a common habit of mind which was sensitive to possible slights, intolerant of apparent loss or defeat, slow to compromise, suspicious of others' motives, and reluctant to admit any advantage to others without a *quid pro quo*. These attitudes operated in many quarters and at various levels, in none perhaps more powerfully than the armed forces. Persistent French naval resentment at British maritime superiority, and military ambition at least to efface earlier defeats whether in Europe, Indo-China or Algeria, contributed greatly to French expansion and territorial aggrandisement. In such a defensive society, the self-centred ambitions of individuals or restricted groups could readily be wrapped in the rhetoric of national interest and security. Often in consequence they could win wide support, as French activity in the Sudan frequently illustrated [92].

Most European governments and many of their citizens shared this concern. In part it was both infectious and self-generating, as, for example, the history of Anglo-French relations demonstrates [83; 118; 119]. Yet watchfulness over prestige also had its sources in domestic assertiveness as well as externally provoked defensiveness. For Italians, the visible asset of colonial territory became important as an acknowledgement of their country's arrival as a nation state. Germans from Bismarck to the Foreign Office official Friedrich von Holstein, and from the Kaiser downwards, were convinced that Britain took an unwarrantably patronising attitude towards their pretensions as a great power; they resented English reluctance to accept that Germany's favour should be cultivated, in part by concessions on colonial issues. The national *amour propre* of 'new' states was a persistently unsettling factor, a spur to global aggrandisement from the late 1870s onwards. By contrast, for the Portuguese an obsessive concern with national prestige was pre-eminently a reflection of their own weakness and vulnerability (in the face of undisguised French, German and British interest in appropriating or at least controlling the development of their colonial possessions), and a reaction to humiliation (e.g. by Britain during the crisis of 1890–1 in India and Central Africa) [67; 81; 86; 132]. The depth of feeling was such that the Portuguese monarchy's survival in the face of republican critics hinged at least on successful defence if not the revitalisation of the empire.

As with diplomatic initiatives, one must ask whether 'prestige' can consistently be seen as providing fundamental impetus to the imperialism of the age. The answer again must surely be 'no'. Clearly imperial acquisitions and influence were widely regarded as necessary to satisfy the desire for international status. But how were colonies and other forms of domination or control capable of providing that satisfaction? Why did it come about at this time that this desire either could or had to be appeased in 'imperial' ways rather than others? Answers to these questions depend on a recognition that diplomatic exchanges often dealt in material coin, and that prestige had its economic buttresses.

In considering the question of prestige, historians inevitably also touch on the broader issues of national or European 'culture' and, ultimately, of nationalism. If we are to understand the dynamics of imperialism, it is necessary to look for ways in which imperatives for overseas expansion were bound up with European societies' widely-accepted sets of values and ideas. Here one is at once brought up against the problem of periodisation, for late nineteenth-century imperialism is quite simply inexplicable in terms only of developments taking place between 1860 and 1914. Two of the powerful urges to intervene beyond Europe and to influence or control both people and territory were the religious – the desire to convert non-Christians to Christianity – and the humanitarian – the wish to better the circumstances of non-Europeans. Even in their modern forms, European humanitarianism, focused above all on slavery and the slave trade, and closely associated with it, the overseas missionary movement, originated chiefly in areas of Protestant religious belief during the second half of the eighteenth century [63; 77; 125]. Earlier Roman Catholic missionary activity had been seriously damaged by the suppression of the Jesuits in 1773. Both movements were dominated until the 1830s almost entirely by Britain and her co-religionists, especially Germans, among Protestant Christians on the continent. After that date, although both drives remained peculiarly powerful in Britain, the benevolent, increasingly paternalistic, view that European intervention would both protect and benefit weaker non-European peoples was widely appealed to.

Virtually from the beginning this 'imperialism of benevolence' was also allied with a strong sense of duty and obligation. Non-European societies were widely seen as poor, ignorant, backward and unprogressive, if not corrupt and degraded, the more so as Europe's own material wealth and technological sophistication rapidly grew [87; 88; 106]. The feeling that Europeans should, or were destined to, pass on the seeds and fruits of their success – their laws, institutions, learning and pre-eminently the Christian religion – was

20

married to the belief that the merits of European ways were self-evident and that their transmission was universally advantageous. From the early nineteenth century there thus existed a powerful sense of Europe's 'mission', secular as well as religious, to the outside world.

These generous but self-righteous and ethnocentric assumptions were part of a genuine sense of European identity, albeit one frequently overshadowed by its separate cultural or national components. Protestants and Roman Catholics, Englishmen, Portuguese and French each rated the others' achievements and offerings far lower than their own. There has been much research into the various European nationalist movements of the nineteenth century, but little comparative evaluation of their strength and impact on the empire-building of our period. What is perhaps clear is that from the 1860s three important developments steadily came together.

First, belief in the easy diffusion of European culture was steadily evaporating in the face of slow progress and apparent resistance from non-Europeans. This produced no serious questioning of basic assumptions but stimulated the search for new methods of transmission and new explanations for the limits to earlier success. Among missionaries, for example, where local societies were resistant or impervious to their message, more began to press for and welcome the use of secular state power to gain an entry, in China in 1858–60, in West and Central Africa from the 1880s [68; 75]. Others argued that failures had resulted from the excessive identification of Christianity with the paraphernalia of western civilisation, and tried to separate the two by extending their activities into areas remote from existing European influences, such as the Congo or inland China [113].

Secondly, from the 1860s the Roman Catholic church began once more to coordinate its own missions overseas. This was at once a sign of the church's recovery from the French revolutionary upheavals, a response to popular religious revival at home, and an aggressive reaction to the expansion everywhere of Protestantism and secular liberal culture [82; 129; 130]. Europe's domestic religious disputes were being rapidly transformed into global rivalries. Churches or denominations, while almost always in theory wary of 'political' involvement, nevertheless often welcomed governments' support where it seemed likely to assist their extra-European ambitions [115].

Humanitarians for their part continued to be preoccupied with the issue of slavery. The disappearance of the trade from the Atlantic in mid-century brought little comfort. Evidence of a flourishing Arab trade in East and Central Africa was provided by mid-century explorers such as the Scottish missionary, David Livingstone. Awareness grew of both the extent of indigenous non-European slavery and the damaging effect of other expanding European 'legitimate' trades, the most noteworthy being those in opium, arms and alcohol. While much investigation remains to be done into these trades and their promoters, the critical response and demands which they provoked for government intervention, control and eradication are very clear [90; 108; 109]. Early nineteenth-century reliance on indirect methods of substituting acceptable or 'legitimate' commerce steadily gave way to appeals for direct territorial control.

The part played by religious and humanitarian networks and ideas between 1860 and 1914 in shaping the outlook on the extra-European world of those not directly engaged in their work has been little studied, but may plausibly be seen as considerable. One of the great staples of popular reading matter after 1860, for example, was provided by the outpourings of the missionary and humanitarian societies, especially in Britain. At the same time, of course, they were not the only opinion-makers. The rapid expansion from the 1830s of Europeans overseas, as settlers, soldiers, merchants, seamen, commercial clerks, officials, hunters, and other travellers or explorers, not only brought back a wealth of additional experience, but also multiplied the numbers of those whose reactions to the non-European world were overwhelmingly self-interested, assertive and narrowly secular.

There is no doubt at all that from mid-century the general outlook of Europeans rapidly became more critically dismissive of other societies, doubtful of non-European capacity for change and progress, and far more readily insistent on their own objectives and inclinations. Such attitudes were certainly not new, but were far more strident and general in our period than ever before. The 'imperialism of obligation', heavily influenced in the early nineteenth century by evangelical Christian hopefulness and a utilitarian optimism, consequently took on an additionally joyless and pessimistic note, illustrated for example in Rudyard Kipling's injunction to 'take up the White Man's burden' [112].

The work of cultural historians has contributed to understanding of this broad development. Older European convictions of superiority were refuelled by consciousness of great material achievements, by awareness of the mounting gulf in terms of wealth and technical capacity. By contrast, Asian societies' apparent decay or stagnation, the seemingly absolute lack of social and material sophistication in African and Pacific communities, only served to heighten Europe's self-esteem. Already by 1860 Karl Marx had defined his Asiatic mode of production, distinguished from the western-inspired ancient, feudal and bourgeois modes as the only one which lacked any inherently progressive tendencies [66].

After that date, Europeans steadily acquired the medical arts of survival in the tropics and learnt to enjoy the opportunities they provided for relaxation and amusement [64; 91; 101; 102]. Memories of mid-century military defeat or barest success, for the French in Algeria or the British in New Zealand and South Africa as late as 1879, were often erased by advances in weaponry and easy victories (albeit with non-European allies) such as Koundian (1889), Segou (1890) and Omdurman (1898). Europeans were consequently struck and frequently irritated by what seemed to them the lukewarm or indefensibly selective enthusiasm shown for these achievements by indigenous peoples, by the latters' lack of deference towards the self-evidently superior and desirable. In the wake of mid-century disasters such as the social and economic decline of the West Indies, the Indian Mutiny (1857) and the Morant Bay Rebellion (1865) in Jamaica, the British in particular associated the mental obtuseness of most non-Europeans with an apparent inability to assimilate and adapt to western ways [72; 74; 124; 138]. As the general European response to the Chinese Boxer uprising or German policies towards the Herero in South-West Africa show, force was widely accepted as the only language readily understood by other races [71;

305]. 'Niggers are tigers' insisted the English Poet Laureate, Alfred Tennyson, in defending Governor Eyre's ruthless suppression of the Jamaican unrest. Such adaptations to western ways as did take place – in Japan, Egypt, Siam or West Africa – were regarded as either eccentric or limited, the bare exceptions to prove the rule.

Instinctive and superficial as these reactions and ideas often were, western scientific hypotheses were increasingly available to provide intellectual underpinning. Applied to human societies, evolutionary explanations of racial differentiation and the mechanism of natural selection seemed to explain and justify cultural differences in terms of inherent racial capacity and a natural hierarchy. In accepting that the 'best' races were also the 'fittest' and would undoubtedly dominate those destined for stagnation or extinction, Europeans endorsed under the label of 'social darwinism' an 'imperialism of inevitability' [5; 123; 314].

Earlier in the nineteenth century, belief in the superiority of European culture was found perfectly compatible with belief in the transferability of that culture to non-Europeans. For many people it imbued the imperial 'mission' with a strong element of obligation to the less fortunate. Once superiority of culture was linked to that of race, a different morality began to influence the practice of European expansion. Assimilation of European and non-European came to seem less desirable and perhaps impossible. Power and superiority rooted in race rather than Providence encouraged a preoccupation with European rights, status and the means of preserving them, which tended to displace older notions of duty, humanitarian benevolence, and ultimate equality. With this shift towards acceptance of a manifest destiny arrived at via inescapable conflict, even the relatively pacific British Prime Minister, Lord Salisbury, could refer without qualms to wars of conquest as froth on the wave of civilisation. Self-exculpation and a search for scapegoats, rather than any questioning of basic assumptions, were the common responses to uncomfortable facts such as Italian defeat by the Abyssinians at Adowa (1896) and Japanese victory over Russia (1905).

While external non-European comparisons bred cultural arrogance and militancy, so too did domestic influences. It can be argued that the development of societies increasingly divided on class lines, a ready acceptance of social conflict and competition, and tolerance if not approval of the hierarchies created, together fostered among all whites an outlook conducive to the subordination or disregard of non-European interests [98]. The growth of professions and white-collar occupations encouraged everywhere the expectation, already for long a part of artisan culture, that skills and status went together and ought to command recognition. Thus the availability of knowledge and technology to Europeans tempted even the coarsest and least able among them to stake claims to superiority, so that ultimately skin-colour itself became a qualification readily accepted in metropolitan Europe as it had long been in colonial societies [76].

The processes by which such views were evolved and propagated are still often obscure. Historians are paying particular attention to the growth of popular and juvenile literature, the expansion of the periodical and newspaper press, and to patterns of schooling [73; 103–105; 117; 121]. Some attach great importance in the British case to the development of competitive sports in conjunction with the expansion of boys' public schools, suggesting that the values developed in such settings readily came to be linked to the importance, acquisition and defence of territorial empire. It has been argued that this represented from about 1880 but one aspect of a wide-ranging campaign of propaganda and persuasion by a limited elite, anxious to generate popular backing for 'an imperial world view, made up of patriotic, military and racial ideas only vaguely located in specific imperial contexts, glorifying violence and a sense of national superiority' [100: 254].

Historians of British expansion appear the most enthusiastic in exploring the interplay of 'cultural' phenomena and imperial dynamism. Clearly the details of Britain's experience are not to be found simply reproduced in Roman Catholic, republican France, or in Prussian-centred, rapidly-industrialising Germany, let alone in Russia. However, such work as has been done, for example on the geographical societies of France and Germany, or on the French newspaper press and literature of empire, is said to point just as it does in Britain to a significant groundswell of popular approval for broadly

25

'imperial' ambitions [65; 121; 122]. It shows an often greater insouciance where non-Europeans were concerned, and a similarly intensifying commitment by 1890 to acquisition and defence of overseas possessions in the face of all comers, not least other Europeans [76; 95].

At this point, it is also appropriate to remember that notions of prestige, self-identity and national interest were given not merely linguistic, ethical or institutional but also militaristic expression. Historians have followed contemporaries in stressing the extent to which after 1870 European states turned to 'militarism', to dramatically increased armaments and an endorsement of military values and achievement as amongst the highest [7; 70; 89; cf.321]. This drew inspiration, of course, from older roots – from traditions of aristocracy and service to the state, historical conflicts, or the imagery of Protestant and Catholic struggles against evil, heathenism and each other. In the late nineteenth century its increased scale heightened the sense of interstate competition, and accentuated feelings of vulnerability at all levels of society. It left governments as much as peoples both willing to act provocatively (even if unwittingly) and easily ruffled. If this outlook is commonly linked with Germany, it was hardly less characteristic of Italy, France, Britain or Russia. Moreover it was everywhere associated, and not only in the minds of intellectuals, with fears of decay or degeneration [111; 123]. The decline of population in France, Britain's impoverished, decrepit urban poor unfit for army life, and Germany's prolific working-class socialists, could all be interpreted as warning signs. As such they stimulated not only state-sponsored programmes of social reform (just as in the 1820s in Britain and 1860s in Germany they had led to plans for state-sponsored emigration), but also enthusiasm for the challenges of sport and war. Playing-field and battle-field frequently merged in the rhetoric of the period. Sturdy populations and expanding empires were mutually supporting, and success in imperial aggrandisement could provide reassurance that all was not yet lost at home. The renewed assertion of nations' imperial missions perhaps offered a counterweight to pessimism, a defence against domestic doubts.

Ideas of benevolence and obligation, beliefs in racial superiority, educational fashions, and martial enthusiasm were readily linked to imperial ambition. They became after 1860 components of what social or cultural historians now refer to as a 'dominant ideology' or the 'culture of imperialism', part cause, part effect of the prevailing expansion and mounting acquisitiveness. Nevertheless, the extent to which those components were necessarily connected, their degree of penetration or pervasiveness within classes or populations, their ultimate importance to the processes of imperialism, remain very contentious questions. All such cultural ingredients were also to be found separated from each other; all found many alternative and arguably more important outlets than support for 'imperialism'. Conflicts over the interpretation of Christian duty or the dictates of benevolence in their bearing on imperialism were constantly recurring. Imperial expansion was often itself looked upon, for example by political leaders like Gladstone or Clemenceau, as a source of military or national enfeeblement, with the dangers of becoming overextended uncomfortably visible. Periodically there was massive popular indifference to the reality of imperialism or empire, which, for different reasons, alarmed both imperial enthusiasts and their critics.

It is easy to exaggerate the extent, coherence and importance of such cultural influences. Opinion and belief were endlessly divided, fickle, and volatile [78]. Undoubtedly the cultural factors discussed here contributed to the broad outlines of Europe's expansion overseas. They assisted in creating the general circumstances within which specific instances of imperial domination, annexation and direct rule became for contemporaries not only imaginable but acceptable. They also shaped the forms of colonialism evolved by different states. It is nevertheless extremely difficult to argue unequivocally that they were direct or proximate causes of Europe's imperialism. Rather than providing the spur to action, cultural self-confidence was no less likely to be the *consequence* of successful imperial assertion, one implication, for example, of the arguments about social imperialism examined below. Appeals to the values of one's own culture or civilisation could provide additional rhetoric, politically or psychologically useful in justifying or legitimising European expansion, conquest and rule. The possession of influence or empire was capable of reinforcing metropolitan assumptions and institutions which had originated in other ways.

A major difficulty for historians, therefore, is that the appeal to cultural phenomena only too often results in the application of sweeping explanations to quite precise forms of imperial activity, with the connection between the two remaining simple-minded or obscure. Quasi-Schumpeterian generalisations about European elites are rarely helpful in explaining why most things happened as and when they did. For example, with Britain only one country among many party to either the partition of Africa or attempts to divide China into spheres of influence, views of the world nurtured by an English public-school education cannot seriously be said to have contributed much to the train of events. No more does the existence of such views help us to explain the widespread British preoccupation with that singular form of empire-building represented by the closer integration of her white-settler Dominions.

These points provide useful counterweights to any interpretation of the period 1860–1914 as one in which the ideological or cultural dynamics of imperialism were uniquely powerful and of primary importance. To raise them, however, is not to deny the significance of social and cultural history. It involves rather a recognition of the substantial degree of autonomy which always existed in the development of ideas and beliefs which were nonetheless sometimes capable of generating imperial commitment and fervour in large numbers of people. Older 'diplomatic' explanations of imperialism have often and rightly been criticised for placing too much reliance on political leaders and other individuals as virtually free agents, unrestricted in choosing the nature, extent and timing of their interventions and expansionist activity. It is equally important to beware the comparable dangers of attributing imperialism to the immersion of individuals in a widespread ideological setting. There is no escape from the need to explore the minds of figures like Cecil Rhodes, Carl Peters, General Gallieni, and King Leopold. It is always essential to dissect carefully the varied springs of individual and group activity, and to examine the many ways in which cultural features derive their life and specific applicability from material circumstances.

# 3 'Metropolitan' Explanations: Social and Economic

Imperialism, especially in the formal acquisition of colonies, involved matters of conscious choice and rational motive, processes in which individuals adopted certain courses of action in preference to others, with a clear sense of the likely consequences. Contemporaries, well aware of the influences touched on in Section 2, often appealed to them as causes of and justifications for imperial expansion. Critics of empire claimed that had other influences or rational arguments from different premises been properly considered, instead of being wilfully ignored by those in positions of power, then entirely different consequences would have followed, bringing the expansion of imperial control to a halt. Many historians have followed this essentially liberal, individualistic form of analysis, concentrating on motive, intention, and personal contacts. However, others have stressed instead the far greater importance for understanding imperialism of the social and economic structures of European societies.

Broadly speaking, these have been seen as decisive in two ways. Some writers have taken an uncompromisingly determinist position, suggesting that contemporary statements about motive or intention can be assigned no more than superficial significance; that government policies as adopted were essentially inescapable; and that imperial dynamics were fundamental reflections of the objective needs of dominant social groups within a particular kind of economic – normally capitalist – system. Others have taken a more relaxed view, arguing that political, ideological, social and economic structures imposed a series of fluctuating constraints on governments, policy-makers and peoples; alternative courses existed, choice and freedom of action were possible, but within rather narrow, shifting limits.

The first of these positions has been associated in the past above all with the cruder forms of Marxist analysis. Most scholars no longer take these very seriously, except as historiographical curiosities, but the fashion still occasionally surfaces from antique intellectual wardrobes. The second approach, the elucidation of structural restrictions and limits on freedom of initiative, has in recent years attracted plenty of attention from historians preccupied with the context in which imperial policies and activities evolved [93; 94; 114; 116]. The general question informing these investigations may be put in the following way: 'at what point did socio-economic structures or conditions become decisive in giving impetus to and in shaping the patterns of imperialism?'

No serious historian denies that deep-seated economic or social changes generated pressures and problems which impelled individuals and groups at many levels to seek solutions involving imperial expansion. This question therefore offers a meeting-place both for liberal historians, weary of too persistent an emphasis on the role of individuals or groups of officials with insufficient reference to pertinent work in social or economic fields, and historians sympathetic to Marxist perspectives yet anxious to turn to account the widest possible range of recent research and criticism. It is at this point that much of the most interesting new work is going on, some of it discussed in Section 5 below. In this section attention is directed mainly to analyses of economic and social changes related to late nineteenth-century imperialism which are not so new, but which continue both to be influential and to raise interesting questions.


**'Social Imperialism'**

The concerns underlying this term were clearly present in all European states by the 1890s, and the concept itself is almost as old, having been used by Marxist analysts *c.*1914 to account for the growth of support for moderate reforming

31

policies and nationalist sympathy in left-wing and working-class circles [156; 205]. The term is now frequently used to refer to circumstances in which a government or political leaders, facing serious domestic social conflicts and possibly disruptive political change as consequences of industrialisation and 'uneven' economic growth, embark on a course of imperial expansion abroad. These expansionist policies are consciously devised to unite the nation and to defuse tensions at home, while simultaneously avoiding significant domestic reform.

As an explanatory concept in this form it was first developed by Hans-Ulrich Wehler, in contributions to debate about both the origins of Bismarck's sudden bid for colonies in Africa and the Pacific during 1884–5, and the developing global policies (*Weltpolitik*) of pre-1914 Germany [133–135]. Wehler portrayed Bismarck as hoping at first to achieve prosperity, contentment, and stability by means of the free-trading commercial expansion widely fashionable in Europe during the 1860s. When this proved unworkable during the economic downturn after 1873, he turned increasingly to devices such as steamship subsidies, discriminatory railway rates, consular support and tariffs. In the 1880s colonies and protectorates provided additional means by which Bismarck, and the pre-capitalist Prussian elite which he represented, capitalised on a mounting Anglophobia plus the popular enthusiasms of pressure-groups such as the *Deutsche Kolonialverein* (German Colonial League), to secure the continued political dominance of a national conservative alliance between industrialists and agrarians. Bismarck thus established a pattern which equally authoritarian successors such as von Bülow and Admiral Tirpitz were to develop with ever greater enthusiasm, striving for continental and even world domination assisted by both formal and informal territorial control.

'Social imperialism' held out the prospect both of conserving the status quo at home, especially by pre-empting radical political change, and of protecting the nation-state externally, associating its security with overseas economic expansion, the acquisition of colonies, and naval power. It was essentially an aggressive policy, consciously adopted and adapted by a ruling elite and designed to manipulate domestic opinion, to mobilise mass support and to divert outwards both liberal or socialist discontents and other pressures for change. Overseas expansion, involving colonial empire, sea power and access to new markets abroad, would generate greater domestic prosperity and make for social stability. Bismarck's imperialism, Wehler argued, established a vital element of continuity in modern Germany's history, in that its foreign policy has always been a response to domestic difficulties, not to external pressures or to any need to defend traditional foreign interests.

Other historians were not slow to point out weaknesses in Wehler's 'social imperialist' analysis. Two main lines of criticism have been developed, the first of which concentrates on the high politics and policy-making of Bismarck and his successors. Even before Wehler's work appeared in English, it had been argued that Bismarck's colonial initiatives, fitful and opportunistic, were not only dictated by short-term calculations of parliamentary expedience but showed the Chancellor acutely aware that in the longer term formal empire, with its costs and responsibilities, could never be of economic or, therefore, of political value. Indeed, Bismarck's attempts to avoid colonial commitments contributed greatly to his downfall in 1890 [210]. In a direct response to Wehler, Paul Kennedy used this to highlight the contrast between Bismarck and his successors, concluding that manipulated social imperialism was only of relevance to the period after 1897 [174]. From then on Berlin's foreign and naval policies were far more consistently designed to direct the popular gaze away from domestic affairs; policies in the Far East and Pacific, calculations about the future of, for example, the Portuguese colonies, all demonstrated an indiscriminate concern for territorial gains and a dogmatic obsession with national standing and prestige. Subsequent analyses have reinforced these reservations, while acknowledging that Germany's foreign policy was also shaped by powerful reactions against the doings of other powers (by fears, for instance, of encirclement inside Europe). 'Bismarck the social imperialist' seems to lack all credibility [39; 110; 163; 164; 175], and although it may always be possible to find advocates 'in all parties . . . making connections between domestic affairs and external policy . . .

it is quite a jump to argue that there was always a primacy of domestic politics' [93: *359*]. Although Wehler's ideas still have their followers in Germany, no more in empire-building than in foreign affairs more broadly conceived do most other historians seem willing to make that jump [19; 69; 168; 188; 208].

The second line of attack, while accepting the concept's utility, nevertheless sees in its single-minded application even to the period after 1897 a gross over-simplification of Germany's history [79; 80]. That history has for too long been presented as both unique in Europe and as all of a piece from Bismarck to Hitler. If less importance is attached to the political dominance of conservative agrarian Prussia and due attention paid instead to the social and economic achievements of the middle classes, the more Germany can be shown to have had in common with its European neighbours. Above all one must recognise the variety of German society, the existence within it of competing nationalisms, and at least two quite distinct meanings given to 'social imperialism'.

On the one hand, there were those conservatives who, although fewer and less significant than Wehler suggests, wished to counteract or neutralise domestic social unrest with no more than a combination of striking successes abroad and nationalistic propaganda at home. By contrast, there were those who, although equally authoritarian in political outlook, believed in a genuine marriage of imperial expansion and social reform; these were the exponents of a radical conservatism akin to that propagated in Britain after 1894–5 by Joseph Chamberlain. Conflict and competition for support between these different groups opened the way for older traditions and other particular interests to influence the pattern of Germany's colonial acquisition and imperial ambitions [164]. 'Social imperialism' alone never provided an adequate explanation for the growth of German empire overseas.

While Wehler's concept was being modified and absorbed into a broader debate about the nature of Germany's recent past, historians of other countries began in the 1970s to look for signs of social imperialism elsewhere. In the realm of public debate these were easily found, as Bernard Semmel had pointed out some years earlier in a study of British social-imperialist thought [205: *ch. 1*; 147]. In British discussion he detected two principal arguments. On one side were those who stressed 'the need to maintain the empire' on whose strength 'the welfare of the working class depended', on the other those emphasising 'the condition of the working classes as the basis of imperialism'. Although in practice these were often combined, the latter – most characteristic of Liberal imperialists – was more directly associated with support for social reform than was the former, the line taken by many tariff reformers after 1903. There are obvious parallels here with the German social-imperial rhetoric, but in Britain such ideas emerged clearly only once territorial expansion was virtually complete, and when priorities lay with the defence and development of Britain's existing empire.

Support is rare for the view that, in the British case, social-imperialist thinking contributed directly to dramatic overseas ventures and even territorial expansion. However, reconsideration of Disraeli's career in the light of Wehler's ideas has led Harcourt to suggest that his imperial commitment rested on precisely these foundations [84]. Economic difficulties in 1866–7 coincided with pressures for political reform and republican agitation; the Abyssinian expedition of 1868 was set in motion to head off the popular demand for change. Here was more, it is claimed, than a mere diversionary tactic or short-lived Palmerstonian extravagance; Disraeli's subsequent endorsement of imperialism and social reform in the 1870s was the natural development of earlier and deeper roots than had previously been recognised. This argument has been challenged in a close analysis of the relevant Foreign Office correspondence, which shows the expedition fitting naturally into a longer-term and far less dramatic pattern of official planning. Nevertheless, Harcourt went on to suggest that Gladstone and his ministers in the early 1870s shared a similar outlook [85; 204; cf.127]. Most scholars, however, seem unconvinced that social imperialist ideas either provided a basis for wide political consensus or carried significant political weight, pointing for evidence to the Liberal election victories in 1868, 1880 and 1906, associated as they were with much anti-imperial rhetoric.

So far historians of France seem to have been more sympathetic than most to the view that the common problems of late nineteenth-century European states – those of managing within an often shaky political system the transition from rural-commercial to heavily urban-industrial societies – produced a common social-imperialist response. It has been argued that this perception of the need for imperial expansion was influential in France even during the late 1870s, and that the establishment of a protectorate over Tunisia in 1881 constituted a fine example of 'social imperialism in action' [157: *esp. ch. 7* and *290–6*]. Certainly in the late 1880s and early 1890s, a new and extended conservative coalition was forged by the conservative republican party of Gambetta, Ferry and Méline. Protectionist tariff policies drew heavy-industrial and agricultural interests together, and the church's political isolation was markedly reduced in that widespread move to reconcile Catholics to the Republic, known as the *Ralliement*. The extension and consolidation of the protected colonial empire, 'in addition to being an effective crutch to the faltering industrial economy, appeared to many Catholic and secular conservatives as an arena for national reconciliation', and thus contributed much to a conscious policy of 'social appeasement without structural reforms' [182: *24–5*].

In France, Elwitt concluded from his examination of the period 1860–84, imperial expansion 'served to consolidate class rule and to insulate the political economy against the shocks generated by the great depression' [157: *310–11*]. Moreover, in the years to 1914, he has argued, French republican objectives paralleled those of Chamberlain in Britain, the architects of the *Sammlungspolitik* in Germany from 1897, and Crispi's coalition in Italy: 'leading ruling-class elements . . . formed a [social-imperialist] consensus to defend order at home and to stake out imperial positions abroad' [158: *289*]. It may well be asked how helpful this formulation actually is. Undoubtedly the extent of the support and degree of unity demonstrated by such groups, and thus their political or economic influence over events, varied greatly from one period or country to another.

At the heart of the social-imperialist *mentalité*, its supporters argue, lay the preoccupation with order, social stability, and political conservatism. Although economic interest groups of many kinds supported the overseas policies of colonial expansion, their own particular profit or even general prosperity were of less importance than the preservation of a social order immune to left-wing challenge. Colonial expansion was valuable above all for the stimulus it gave to a sense of national unity and acceptance of the status quo, rather than the swelling of company accounts, although that too would be welcome if it happened. If colonial successes could breed domestic social and political legitimacy then they were welcome, even if the price by other standards was high.

The term 'social imperialism' might indeed be used to denote all instances where imperial expansion can be presented primarily as 'a reaction of political elites forced to do something to save their privileged position when the social basis of their power shrank or was endangered as a result of socio-economic change' [27:3]. Quite evidently sections of Russia's governing elites felt this sense of embattlement and loss of credibility between 1860 and 1914. For them, as for comparable groups in both Italy under Giolitti and Portugal especially in the 1890s, new or revitalised expansion held out at least one of the keys to their survival, with its promise of reducing the sense of backwardness or failure engendered by the activities of other powers. However, it is difficult to determine whether 'social' imperialism might have been overtaken by, or was ever more than a cloak for, other more precise concerns. Historians of Italy have rejected social imperialism, favouring either a theatrical imperialism tied to images of national and great power status, or an 'industrial imperialism' confined to the period after 1907. This not only has much in common with the emphasis of some recent French historiography [20; 145; 217]. The concept seems also to have found little favour with scholars intent on defining the concerns of newly-emerging elites.

What precise explanatory power the concept of 'social imperialism' retains is therefore far from clear. Its very attractions – a recognition that there were widely-shared European problems of social and political adjustment to the growth of modern industrial economies; its scepticism about stark divisions of internal from external policy or of political from economic history – surely have a correlative weakness in their

37

essential generality. To what extent did 'social imperialism' really represent something more, or a conscious commitment greater, than the sum of its parts? Was it ever more than an ambiguous or rhetorical device of politicians anxious to devise temporary platforms? At best, perhaps, it may help to explain why colonies and expansion in general prospect came to seem at least to some people either desirable or acceptable. A great deal more research into the outlooks and alliances of business-men, landed and labouring classes may nevertheless be neces-sary if we are to assess its importance in this respect. It is more certain that social imperialism, however defined, cannot explain either the possibility of individual colonial acquisitions or the precise direction and timing of colonial initiatives by imperial powers.

### 'Economic Imperialism'

The importance of economic interests and calculation in the expansion of European influence and control over the extra-European world is undeniable. Equally unexceptionable is the general observation that this expansion in the late nineteenth and early twentieth centuries coincided with marked if uneven growth, major transformations associated with indus-trialisation or urbanisation, and striking fluctuations in the economies of European states [181; 199; 213; 310–312]. The intellectual incentive to find the fundamental impetus to empire-building in Europe's economic development and in the wider extension of a world economy, has long been powerful. It has been encouraged further by awareness of the development of imperial ambitions in both the United States and Japan as industrialisation took a firm hold at the end of the nineteenth century [143; 206; 211].

Explanations of Europe's supposed avidity for empire and colonies have therefore frequently placed great weight on par-ticular economic factors or interests. They have variously emphasised the needs of western capitalism as a system embracing all the imperial powers, the individual character and fluctuations of national economies, the changing economic position of states relative to their chief rivals, and the role of either separate economic sectors or clusters of firms and entrepreneurs. Elements of all four can be found, for example, in the analyses of 'social imperialism' referred to in the previous section, where the political and social uncertainties of the period have been presented as products of the difficulties affecting wide sectors of European industry and agriculture during the so-called 'Great Depression' (1873–96). The secondary literature on the economics of empire-building is staggering in its extent, and is already the subject of valuable general surveys, both bibliographical and analytical [3; 10; 302; 303].

Taking their cues from the halting and patchy but nonetheless inexorable expansion of industrial capitalism, and from the conclusions of early commentators, historians have long concentrated on the idea that empire served three basic requirements. In an age of growing population, the rise of employment in manufacturing and services, and the relative decline of agriculture, colonies could supply demands for food and raw materials often no longer capable of being met from home. The prospect of Asian-grown cotton and silk or African mineral supplies was welcomed. Secondly, with huge increases in the scale and output of industry, freer or more extended trade with extra-European peoples (particularly perhaps with those contained in one's own colonies) could provide the markets needed to absorb the greater production. Latin America's and China's potential consumption of imported manufactures seemed to many self-evidently vast. Moreover, cheaper raw materials and larger markets were required to offset the general fall in prices from the 1870s to the 1890s; with most industrial powers adopting protectionist tariffs, colonies could serve both needs. Finally, the possibilities for development, and the need of the extra-European world for all manner of facilities from urban housing to railways, opened up vast opportunities for the investment overseas of Europe's savings or 'surplus' capital. In an age of escalating competition and international tension, colonial supplies, markets and investments were sometimes assumed to be more secure than those in independent countries which one did not control.

In so far as they applied to formal colonies, these suppositions gradually lost much of their superficial plausibility in the face of detailed research and accumulated statistical evidence. With few exceptions colonial trade remained throughout this period an insignificant proportion of metropolitan commerce. Most colonial markets grew only slowly and it was rare for a country's colonial commodities to outweigh alternative sources of supply. The exceptions tended to be British, where some 25 per cent of the nation's import and export trades was imperial. Yet even this was virtually accounted for by Canada, Australia, India and, after 1890, South Africa – in the main longstanding possessions rather than creations of any later nineteenth-century expansionism, and, in the case of the white settlement colonies, territories rapidly distancing themselves from metropolitan controls.

Europe's long-term overseas investment also went overwhelmingly to areas outside the formal colonial empires. French capital went to Russia, Italy's to the Balkans and Middle East, British to the United States and Latin America, German to all of these areas [146; 151; 154; 163]. While British investors looked comparatively favourably on the white settlement colonies as a whole, preference shifted markedly from one period to another. New Zealand was regarded as insecure after 1880, and Australia's reputation did not recover from the slump of 1890–2. Canada's great popularity came after 1900 and was matched by the equally powerful attractions of Argentina [151; 196; 200]. Metropolitan perceptions of global investment risks and opportunities were the decisive factor, and the newer spheres of interest or formal annexations were in practice rated poorly. Even older possessions derived little benefit or preference from colonial status in attracting funds. (See Table 1.)

These features were part reflection, part cause, of the fact that the interest of most metropolitan business in overseas expansion was also limited and intermittent. This view of course is hotly disputed. Early Marxist critics linked imperialism to the growth of 'monopoly capitalism' in the leading sectors of European economies, and some contemporary historians see in Hilferding's 'organised capital' or Bukharin's 'state capitalism' concepts worth re-examining [307]. Imperialism has been equated with a form of 'finance capitalism',

**Table 1**
**A. Geographical distribution of British long-term capital investment overseas (1913)**

| Within the empire | Millions of pounds | Outside the empire | | Millions of pounds |
|---|---|---|---|---|
| Canada and Newfoundland | 514.9 | The United States | | 754.6 |
| Australia and New Zealand | 416.4 | Argentina | 319.6 | |
| South Africa | 370.2 | Brazil | 148.0 | |
| West Africa | 37.3 | Mexico | 99.0 | |
| India and Ceylon | 378.8 | Chile | 61.0 | |
| Straits Settlements | 27.3 | Uruguay | 36.1 | |
| British North Borneo | 5.8 | Peru | 34.2 | |
| Hong Kong | 3.1 | Cuba | 33.2 | |
| Other colonies | 26.2 | Remainder Latin-America | 25.5 | |
| | 1,780.0 | Total Latin-America | | 756.6 |
| | | Russia | 110.0 | |
| | | Spain | 19.0 | |
| | | Italy | 12.5 | |
| | | Portugal | 8.1 | |
| | | France | 8.0 | |
| | | Germany | 6.4 | |
| | | Austria | 8.0 | |
| | | Denmark | 11.0 | |
| | | Balkan States | 17.0 | |
| | | Rest of Europe | 18.6 | |
| | | Total Europe | | 218.6 |
| | | Egypt | | 44.9 |
| | | Turkey | | 24.0 |
| | | China | | 43.9 |
| | | Japan | | 62.8 |
| | | Rest of foreign world | | 77.9 |
| | | Total | | 1,983.3 |
| | | Grand Total | | 3,763.3 |

**Table 1 (*continued*)**
**B. Geographical distribution of French long-term foreign investment (1900; 1914)**

| (Billions of francs) | | | |
|---|---|---|---|
| *1900* | | *1914* | |
| Russia | 7.0 | Russia | 11.3 |
| Turkey (in Asia and Europe) | 2.0 | Turkey (in Asia and Europe) | 3.3 |
| Spain and Portugal | 4.5 | Spain and Portugal | 3.9 |
| Austria-Hungary | 2.5 | Austria-Hungary | 2.2 |
| Balkan states | 0.7 | Balkan states | 2.5 |
| Italy | 1.4 | Italy | 1.3 |
| Switzerland, Belgium, and Netherlands | 1.0 | Switzerland, Belgium, and Netherlands | 1.5 |
| Rest of Europe | 0.8 | Rest of Europe | 1.5 |
| Total Europe | 19.9 | Total Europe | 27.5 |
| French colonies | 1.5 | French colonies | 4.0 |
| Egypt, Suez, and South Africa | 3.0 | Egypt, Suez, and South Africa | 3.3 |
| United States and Canada | 0.8 | United States, Canada, and Australia | 2.0 |
| Latin-America | 2.0 | Latin-America | 6.0 |
| Asia | 0.8 | Asia | 2.2 |
| Grand Total | 28.0 | Grand Total | 45.0 |

**C. Geographical distribution of German long-term foreign investment (1914)**

| (Billions of marks) | | | |
|---|---|---|---|
| *Europe* | | *Outside Europe* | |
| Austria-Hungary | 3.0 | Africa (including German colonies) | 2.0 |
| Russia | 1.8 | | |
| Balkan countries | 1.7 | Asia (including German colonies) | 1.0 |
| Turkey (including Asiatic Turkey) | 1.8 | United States and Canada | 3.7 |
| France and Great Britain | 1.3 | Latin-America | 3.8 |
| Spain and Portugal | 1.7 | Other areas | 0.5 |
| Rest of Europe | 1.2 | | |
| | 12.5 | | 11.0 |

*Source*: Herbert Feis, *Europe The World's Banker, 1870–1914* (New York, W.W. Norton, 1965 edn) pp. 23, 51, 74.

for example, in recent analyses of French banking and industrial groups acting closely with the state in policies towards China and the Ottoman empire after 1900 [17; cf.175; 182]. Nevertheless, the diffuse nature of banking and finance, and the continuing high degree of separation of industrial, banking and commercial organisation, meant that there was little concentration of European domestic business interest in imperial expansion. This can be highlighted in several ways.

Those most strident advocates of empire – the various colonial movements consisting of bodies like the *Deutsche Kolonialverein*, the *Gesellschaft für deutsche Kolonization*, or the French *'parti coloniale'* with its subgroups such as the *Comité de l'Asie Française*, and the navy leagues in Britain and Germany – were very small in numbers. Their ranks were full of middle-class professionals – journalists, politicians, academics and representatives of the armed forces – but they attracted relatively few businessmen [69; 136–139; 194]. A particularly full breakdown has been made of the French movement, concluding that the *'parti coloniale'* represented the highest stage not of French capitalism but of French nationalism' [136: *148*; 140; 193]. Colonialists everywhere wanted business support, to provide them with funds and to build up the empire, but such links as were forged tended to be short-lived. They were also vitiated by the tendency of colonialists to use economic arguments to drum up support rather than because they attached importance to them *per se*, and by the willingness of business to operate both indiscriminately across colonial boundaries and in cooperation with the nationals of other rival powers.

Most firms simply wanted access and security for whatever investment was made; they cared little who provided them as long as it was done effectively and cheaply. Businessmen were very willing to put pressure on their governments, normally through their local chambers of commerce, when these basic interests seemed to be threatened in any way. Work on the British chambers of commerce has been growing, revealing important conclusions [170; 171; 203; 207]. The internal politics of individual chambers often meant that members lent their names to resolutions demanding action, while having no direct interest in the issue. Requests for intervention commonly fell far short of a desire for one's own government to assume direct control; short-term consular action, diplomatic negotiations to mitigate the protectionist commercial policies of another power, support for railway or telegraph building were far more often sought. The uproar surrounding the Anglo-Portuguese treaty of February 1884 provides an interesting case-study in this respect. With Manchester merchants in the lead, British chambers of commerce forced the abandonment of an agreement which threatened to entrench Portuguese control and thus the danger of protective tariffs at the mouth of that potentially great commercial highway, the Congo River [141].

The timing of agitations by chambers of commerce tended, moreover, to coincide with downturns in trading conditions and the (often associated) protectionist moves of Portugal and France [69; 170; 171; 207]. British chambers were unusually worried on this score in the mid-1880s and again in the early 1890s. By their nature, however, such agitations were usually also short-lived. Not only could an improvement in local conditions remove the need for action. Work on West Africa, one of the principal areas of concern, suggests that merchants were frequently more adaptable than was previously realised; they probably attached less importance in practice to the possibility of government action on their behalf than their rhetoric might suggest [192; see also 184]. Governments, aware of both this short-term outlook and the conflicting views of different chambers, were frequently able to ride out protests until confidence recovered. Positive official responses to commercial pressures might be either delayed until elections were in sight (Britain in 1892) or entirely dependent on the accident of personality (as when Joseph Chamberlain became Colonial Secretary in 1895).

Official action might appear as a response to commercial pressure when in fact it was driven by quite other concerns. The patchiness of metropolitan economic interests in empire-building made it possible for governments to be highly selective in responding to economic pressure and demands by private enterprise, just as the multiplicity of their other domestic and international concerns made it politically necessary. Businessmen and government officials tried quite unabashedly to exploit each other's interests and resources their own ends, and this habit increased after 1880 as tne relationship between political influence and economic activity grew more direct in many parts of the extra-European world. From time to time coincidences of interest made cooperation possible and bred imperial control.

The best-known examples of these coincidences, the late nineteenth-century chartered companies which were originally welcomed by governments as a fairly informal means of control, have been thoroughly studied [144; 214; 153; 159; 162; 165; 166; 189; 150; 191; 215]. The processes by which such fragile combinations of political authority and economic interest collapsed almost everywhere and were replaced by direct imperial rule, are also now well understood. The Royal Niger Company, granted a charter in 1886, within only two years alienated the other British merchants by restrictive practices contrary to the spirit of its grant. While Salisbury's ministry was prepared to play down these abuses, whitewash became more difficult to apply. Outraged traders sacked the Company's headquarters at Akassa in 1895, and the Company failed to deter subsequent French advances from the north. It was eventually relieved of its powers by 1900. German companies were still less successful: the German East Africa Company, for example, almost immediately provoked the Swahili-Arab Abushiri uprising of 1888–9 and was equally swiftly replaced by direct rule. The Portuguese Mozambique Company survived, but for many years remained utterly feeble and impoverished.

However, these were not alone as examples of European governments' attempts to create informal empires, in which by virtue of their support for private commercial and financial ambitions they exercised a measure of control without (at least in theory) the inconvenience of responsibility. The governments of Turkey, Persia and China relied more and more on borrowing heavily abroad and in consequence had to open their countries to European concessionaires. In such areas of limited commercial importance but exaggerated potential, Germany, France, Britain and Russia all competed for the political influence required to defend their various strategic, geo-political and prestigious concerns. They did so perforce by supporting carefully-selected banking, railway and other metropolitan enterprises in key sectors of the local economies, sometimes on an exclusively national basis, at others in international ventures [142; 155; 176; 183; 186–188; 212]. Such strategies had mixed success, even before the war of 1914–18 turned the world upside down. British efforts to gain influence at Germany's and Russia's expense in Persia and Turkey fell apart before 1914. Both there and in the Far East, where Europe's spheres of influence had slightly more reality, the presence of competing European powers sometimes restored the initiative to local authorities able to exploit Europe's rivalries.

Given the restricted and diffuse nature of imperially directed business and investment before 1914, it is not surprising that many historians have been reluctant to formulate grand generalisations about economics and empire, and have instead pursued more narrowly focused enquiries. Many of the questions being asked in such studies are not unfamiliar. Which economic interests – firms, regions, sectors – were more or less weighty, and in what periods were they individually influential? How independent of or reliant on other imperial dynamics were they? What part did they play in the calculations of those in a position to commit the powers and resources of metropolitan governments to the support of individual ventures, economic sectors or a 'national economy'?

New lines of investigation, however, can produce striking results. For example, fresh scrutiny of the sources for Britain's overseas investment figures has prompted a hefty downward revaluation of the sums involved [197; 198]. If correct, this will not only require a reassessment of the relative importance of the economic components of Britain's imperialism; it also suggests that increased importance should be attached to local contributions to imperial growth and colonial development [225]. Revaluation is linked to the argument that London, rather than handling largely British-generated funds, may have acted as a channel for continental European funds moving abroad, to an extent hitherto quite unrealised. These ideas are currently in dispute [160], but at least suggest that the relation of Europe's capital exports with empire-building requires reassessment.

46

Some attention has been given to the imperial interests of particular localities. Work on port cities has a long pedigree, but is still being added to and many other centres would benefit from further study, such as Lisbon, Barcelona, Aberdeen or Manchester [185; 216]. Among French cities, the African and Asian links of Marseilles and Bordeaux are well known. The interest of Lyon and especially its silk industry in the Indo-China trade has also been thoroughly examined. This prompted the invention of a generic term, 'municipal imperialism', to signify these particular urban and commercial lobbies, along with the suggestion that the French tradition of local historical studies could be profitably extended by historians to shed more light on imperial connections [177–179; 245].

Studies of businesses with colonial and imperial ties have also multiplied in recent years. Unfortunately, many of these are very inward-looking. They fail to address the questions of domination and control or the relations with imperial authority which concern historians of imperialism, but some important work has emerged. Stimulating suggestions as to the relation of distinct economic and political 'partitions' of Africa, and the role therein of expatriate European firms, are no less relevant to other parts of the globe [169]. Research into the expansion of mining and related industries in southern Africa has thrown much light on several critical areas – the contribution of entrepreneurial ambition to the territorial expansion of direct colonial control, the contacts of businessmen with government officials, the composition of business networks, and the range of European investment in the region [285; 316: *854–67*]. Interpretations remain deeply divided over the central questions either of the degree to which imperial policies were the outcome of successful pressure by business, or of the extent to which businessmen and officials simply shared common or complementary outlooks significant in shaping 'the pattern of imperialism'.

In other types of enterprise, notably trade and shipping, the relationship between business and government could often be unequivocally adversarial as well as distant. Shipping firms in particular demonstrated a capacity for taking government contracts while at the same time operating shipping conferences which benefited themselves and foreign rivals at the expense of national interest [201; 202]. Study of trade and shipping connections has also revealed what so far seems to have been an essentially British form of enterprise, the investment house, forerunners in many respects of present-day multinational companies. These commercial firms were often based outside London and were entirely independent of the metropole and its capital market, but they were responsible for large numbers of subsidiary joint-stock companies, reinvesting their own local profits and tapping capital widely throughout Asia and Australasia. William Mackinnon's British India Steam Navigation Company and its associated firms, for instance, can be seen not only as an interesting and complex example of expatriate enterprise, but as one which was able at different times to establish a wide variety of links with both the imperial and Indian colonial governments [173; 190]. The complexity of such investment groups (as they have been christened), the cosmopolitan nature of ostensibly British imperial firms (such as the Hong Kong and Shanghai Bank with its steady complement of German directors, links to German interests, and independence of London), and the 'subimperialisms' of remote expatriate and settler enterprise, all confirm that there was nowhere any 'simple or unambiguous' connection between capitalist business and imperial enterprise [152: *112*; 148; 149; 172; 195].

Firms of every kind struggled to find or create a congenial environment, and could never rely either on a colonial setting or on their own national governments or investors to provide it. It was for that reason that William Lever established his oil plantations in the Congo rather than British West Africa. It remains to be seen to what extent this same variety, mobility and cosmopolitanism was characteristic of German, French and other European enterprise. In French, German and Belgian Africa, imperial governments, once they had made good their political claims, adopted a definite policy of granting concessions in order to spread development and to consolidate their rule [150; 153; 159; 161; 218]. Although the generally lamentable record of such companies is plain enough, little is yet known about the developing relationships of more than a handful of concession-seekers, concessionaires and government officials in such centres as Brussels, Paris and Lisbon, let alone Rome or St Petersburg [191; 209; 215].

These discussions of individual companies or business sectors immediately confront historians with some basic problems in offering explanations of imperialism. They remind one forcefully of the difficulty in linking structural constraints or pressures such as European economic depression, over-production, price falls, social unrest, and domestic political challenges, to the thinking and action of those responsible for political or administrative decisions about national policy. It creates an awareness both of immense variety and of the danger of generalising about global phenomena from a limited range of examples. Moreover the difficulties which entrepreneurs faced in sustaining their enterprises overseas also draw our investigations inexorably away from the European metropole to the conditions which actually confronted governments, businessmen and others overseas.

# 4 'Peripheral' Explanations

By the 1860s, a marked feature of Europe's expansion was the presence abroad of large numbers of her nationals – traders, civilian officials, missionaries, settlers and armed forces. Their activities often bred conflicts, with one another, between individuals of different nationalities, and with local indigenous people. The expansion of European activity – whether by continental consolidation overland, as in the Russian or analogous North American cases, or overseas – produced many ill-defined, unstable and 'turbulent' frontiers. These tensions were hardly inevitable, but proved only rarely containable locally, and could not be permanently ignored by metropolitan agencies [220; 226; 230; 233]. Threats to local authorities who failed to maintain impartial and effective control, direct intervention, the often violent assertion of European power, and finally forms of annexation and the permanent extension of colonial rule, frequently followed.

It is now accepted as a commonplace that the patterns of imperialism have never been dictated solely by forces originating inside Europe which were then simply transmitted abroad. Europeans taking steps to intervene in or to control other territories and peoples can more often than not be seen as having responded to distant, developing situations over which they had little influence, and which seemed at the time to offer them few alternative courses of action. It is hardly ever possible to separate entirely 'peripheral' from 'metropolitan' influences, but 'peripheral' explanations of imperialism have tended to emphasise the reluctance of many Europeans, especially of governments, to become involved in any way formally overseas. Their indifference or reluctance were overcome only as they found themselves unable to resist the pull of local crises and became afraid to risk the consequences of non-intervention. By their very nature 'peripheral' explanations can seem to make effective generalisations extremely difficult, given the immense range of local confrontations between an expanding Europe and the non-European world.

'Peripheral' or, as they are sometimes called, 'excentric' explanations of late nineteenth-century imperial expansions were especially prominent in the literature from about 1960 until the early 1980s. There were several reasons for this. The end of Europe's colonial empires, the rapidity of decolonisation after 1945 under the pressure as it seemed of colonial nationalists, created a climate in which the scholarly study of non- or extra-European history flourished in its own right, not simply as an extension of European activity abroad. The power of non-Europeans to affect European decisions and courses of action seemed more and more decisive, and it was natural to consider how this had operated in earlier periods.

For historians of imperialism, striking confirmation of the great importance and explanatory value of 'peripheral' perspectives was provided by the work of R.E. Robinson and J.A. Gallagher [239; 240]. For them, the crucial determinants lay in the nature of local societies – in their stability and economic competence, in their ability and willingness to adjust to the slow penetration of European interests and influence, in their capacity to take up European modes of organisation and technology [241–243; cf. 234], and in the extent to which their development or reactions ran counter to important, often non-economic, European interests. European dynamics and initiatives were thus discounted, and the terms 'local crisis', non-European 'collaboration' and 'resistance', gained wide currency [240].

Further reinforcement of this approach came from the findings of much non-European history. Perceptions of imperial rule changed as belief in Europe's power to impose order and to direct change was replaced by, first, an acute sense of the limited impact of much colonial rule, and, subsequently, an awareness of Europeans' extensive, continuing dependence on local personnel or institutions. Historians therefore concluded that imperialism could be properly understood only if they fully appreciated the local circum-

51

stances and the societies being dominated or colonised. In place of imperialism regarded as a straightforward or uni-linear process of Europe's mounting intrusion, assertion of influence or control, and then perhaps conquest, there developed an awareness of the fluctuating interaction of societies and governments on both sides, a process in which there existed a far greater equality both of power between European and non-European, and of ability on both sides to determine outcomes, than had previously been recognised [e.g. 238; 248].

Robinson's and Gallagher's classic exposition of the 'peripheral' interpretation focused on Africa and Britain's acquisition of extensive territory there between 1875 and 1900 [239; 240]. European expansion – notably trade, capital investment, and settlers – provoked serious instability and conflict at the two ends of the continent, Egypt and South Africa. Conditions of 'local crisis' were confirmed when in both regions vigorous criticism of and resistance to the European or British presence crystallised in what were labelled (sometimes by contemporaries as well as recent historians) 'nationalist' movements. These movements, intent on curbing foreign influence or presence, could not be ignored because they seemed to jeopardise Britain's national interest in the security of the two great routes to India and the East via Suez or the Cape of Good Hope. Britain felt obliged to intervene lest those hostile to her – Boers, supporters of Arabi Pasha, another power such as France or Russia – obtain local political control. British intervention in turn both provoked resentment on the part of other Europeans and fanned the 'nationalist' flame, so causing the scramble for territory to snowball, and the British themselves to participate more vigorously as their defensive frame of mind hardened.

From the start aspects of this analysis met vigorous and effective criticism. In particular West Africa sat ill with an interpretation which attached little importance to commercial conflicts and rivalry, played down a history of expanding European intervention and control which long preceded the Egyptian crisis of 1881–2 [245], and minimised local processes of empire-building peculiar to that region. It was shown how changing terms of trade generated local conflicts:

between British and French officials anxious about colonial revenues and the costs of disorder in their existing coastal footholds; between European merchants of different national- ities keen to protect at least their existing spheres; and between those same officials or merchants and African traders, notably the powerful middlemen of the coast depen- dent for their own livelihoods on controlling European access to the interior [228]. The piecemeal assertion of European authority, with or without a measure of African consent, being more and more evidently inadequate to the situation, appeals to Paris or London often seemed hard to refuse. Metropolitan intervention – at last, perhaps, an 'informal imperialism' – gathered ground in the 1870s and 1880s [83; 171; 227; 232; 235; 236].

To the struggle for secure profit or revenue and depend- able if not favourable trading conditions was added, for example, the military expansionism of French forces in Senegal and the western Sudan. There, local governors and commanders from Faidherbe in the 1860s to Archinard in the 1890s, exploited with ingenuity and breathtaking insubor- dination the confused institutions and politics of the Third Republic in support of their sustained local wars and con- quests. These were directed at powerful neighbouring rulers such as Ahmadu and Samori Touré, and were justified by appeals to French security [92]. Missionary enterprise consti- tuted a further agency of European penetration. Protestants and Roman Catholics, such as the British Church Missionary Society and the Société des Missions Africaines, not only encouraged an unsettling degree of cultural change but, even by their mere presence, often held out support and encour- agement to potential allies, thereby greatly exacerbating both internal political divisions and interstate conflicts [68; 82; 219]. For missionaries as for merchants older collaborative arrangements began to break down in the 1870s and 1880s, restricting their areas of access and threatening their security. As first tariffs and then further locally negotiated treaties failed, recovery of that earlier freedom and prospects for future expansion seemed increasingly to depend on territorial gains and overall effective European control. In the 1890s, once the fragility of the arrangements devised at the Berlin

West African Conference (Nov. 1884–Jan. 1885) was exposed, the European powers used every possible means to assert their claims [227].

This West African work and other subsequent research has been significant in two ways, for the interpretation of Africa's partition and for 'peripheral' explanations in general. In rejecting the argument that local crisis in Egypt held the key to Britain's and, in large part, European imperial expansion as a whole in Africa, it did not of course abandon the idea that 'peripheral' or local factors critically influenced the pattern of imperialism. Rather was the reverse true. The separate regional components of Africa began to assume greater individual and explanatory importance in the history of the continent's partition, and the range of significant local dynamics was increased. There emerged a larger selection of 'men on the spot', individuals capable of committing the power and prestige or political fortunes of metropolitan governments without prior sanction and beyond the possibility of disavowal [223]. The independent power of interest groups – in Africa, for example, the French *troupes coloniales*, white Cape or Natal settlers, East Africa's Asians – anxious to promote their own 'subimperialism' was more readily appreciated [cf. 225; 247]. Moreover, it was seen that in the British case the metropolitan 'official mind', both in understanding the significance and in responding to the ripples of local activity, was far less assured and single-minded than had apparently been implied by the weight originally attributed to its strategic preoccupations in Robinson and Gallagher's *Africa and the Victorians*.

Historians' understanding of Africa's partition, that most obviously dramatic example of imperialism in motion during our period, has shifted as a result. The emphasis placed on the defence of open access and commercial opportunity has helped to an appreciation of the central role played by Leopold II of the Belgians, his International Association, and the establishment of his Congo Free State [246]. Leopold's ambitions offered the other powers an answer to their fears that the power vacuum in much of central and western Africa might be filled by a serious European rival. The establishment of his Congo Free State, blessed with international approval, committed to humanitarian goals as well as to the study of Africa, and guaranteeing open access plus complete freedom of trade, enabled interested parties at least temporarily to square their own material self-interest with concern for the benefit and well-being of Africans. In the south the local white expansionism, especially of the Cape's settler and commercial society, has been portrayed as perhaps sufficiently powerful on its own to set southern Africa largely aside from the processes of partition at work elsewhere in the continent [244].

More generally, the term 'local crisis' has lost much of its precision both chronologically and in content. 'Crisis' is in any case an over-used word, but the final confrontation or point of decisive intervention and annexation has steadily been overshadowed by the sense of cumulative tension and progressive erosion of local societies' strength and stability on various fronts. The process of western penetration, often from different directions simultaneously, is given more prominence than either the occasion of final breakdown or the immediate issue at stake [120; 229; 231].

This widening perspective seems likely to encourage two further consequences. In explaining the metropolitan response to 'peripheral' developments, historians can more easily argue that a 'national' range of interests was at stake, where they have previously stressed the key role of narrowly official reactions rather than the influence of more extensive unofficial pleadings. Thus, in the case of Egypt, protection of British or French trade, investment and banking might be preferred to an emphasis on the role of national defence and strategy [229]. Secondly, students of Europe's history, not just those of the extra-European world, will have to develop further their understanding of the many changes induced in non-western states and societies, which were adapting to or trying to contain western influences through such means as constitutional or legal change, interstate alliances and rearmament. This will intensify the tendency of 'peripheral' perspectives, as handled by some scholars, towards an insistence on interaction and a greater equality of influences from both sides in explanatory accounts of imperialism [cf. 222].

Although Africa has provided the setting for much of the

most influential modern work on the 'peripheral' impetus behind Europe's imperialism, these kinds of explanation for domination and annexation are applicable everywhere. Naval captains, consuls or colonial governors could be involved in conflicts of political authority; missionaries could be murdered; traders might be criminals, fraud victims or subject to trade stoppages; wittingly or unwittingly local customs could be slighted and sensitivities outraged, regardless of period, place or nationality. European economic trends, such as the price falls or impact of steam shipping on trading practices transmitted from the metropoles in the 1870s and 1880s, were no more intelligible or acceptable to non-European traders in Indo-China than in West Africa. The internal or external conflicts of Central Asian khanates or Malayan sultanates, which created difficulties for their neighbours and those with whom they had dealings, are again examples of a phenomenon endlessly repeated.

Non-European societies experiencing such pressures and disturbances varied in their capacity to handle them [180; 195]. The surrender of authority associated, for example, with the Egyptian capitulations or Chinese treaty ports, the social and economic imbalances brought about by the rise of new entrepreneurial groups or by labour migration involving Indians, Chinese or Pacific islanders, the perceived threats to custom and beliefs raised everywhere by the acceptance of western ideas or conversion to Christianity, were all seriously unsettling. Added to long-existing or independent internal motors for change, these developments could contribute to political upheaval and breakdown, or perhaps spawn resistance to Europeans and a new, possibly 'nationalist', cohesion. Although some significant groups, like the Mandarins serving the Manchu regime or Wahabi fundamentalists in the Islamic world, resisted alien influences, few societies set their face against all accommodation with European interests, for the reason that in most there were influential groups convinced the west had something to offer them. All were at first confident that they could control the western impact, choosing what they wanted – education, capital, political alliances, or consumer goods – and rejecting the rest. The degree of European penetration in different areas was not only a measure of European interest but reflected the varying strength of these non-European convictions and readiness to cooperate [221; 241; 243; cf. 236]. Even before 1900, many Africans and Asians had taken advantage of a western education either in mission schools or abroad in Europe or the USA, but were also emerging as potent critics of the western impact on their worlds [68; 295:*chs 2–3*].

In many parts of the world and at various levels of activity, as already noted, these changes and the willingness to compromise invited a European response. Case-studies now abound which illustrate the rising degree of European intervention and control in search of local conditions both favourable to their interests and likely to last. Some historians go so far as to detect in the accumulation of instability and confrontation a 'general crisis' in relations between Europe and the extra-European world during the 1880s and 1890s, and suggest that the extent of imperial intervention depended on the ability of other societies to respond to that crisis in mutually acceptable ways. It has been widely accepted following Robinson's influential essay on 'collaboration', that the pattern of imperialism, the diverse spectrum of informal and formal imperial relations, 'was as much and often more a function of Afro-Asian politics than of European politics and economics' [241: *138–9*].

In one of the most influential accounts [3], it is argued that peripheral conflicts of interest were of course not new, even though more common after 1870 because of improved communications, exploration and expanding economic activity. All European governments continued after 1870 as before to employ both formal and informal means of resolving them. Conflicts of specifically economic interest were generally soluble by informal means and in no way necessarily required solution by formal control; only if the problem had become in some way 'political', by definition therefore less amenable to informal solutions, was formal rule or annexation adopted and even then only as a last resort. Finally, 'By definition peripheral explanations . . . deal in specific events [and] cannot form the basis for any general theory of imperialism. At most, observation of recurrent patterns may justify the conclusion that since many peripheral problems stemmed from the same broad expansion of European activities they had common features and required similar remedies' [3: 77].

In contemplating 'peripheral' explanations, however, it is important to be aware of certain pitfalls. As Fieldhouse's work suggests, they can seem ultimately to back away not only from any 'general theory' (which is probably wise) but from any systematic approach to imperialism [224]. Redirecting attention away from the characteristic details of European states and economies carries with it two dangers. The first is that Europe will be regarded as homogeneous, generally confident, steadily expanding and uniformly 'capitalist', which it was not. Secondly, disorder at the periphery arising from that expansion will be reduced to no more than the failure or breakdown of political authority, requiring only the substitution of more powerful and experienced government in the form of European rule, to recreate an order in everyone's interests. That is a gross oversimplification, which even the briefest consideration of European relations with, say, China should indicate [155; 183; 315]. It is not enough to say that in the 'most general terms . . . Europe was pulled into imperialism by the magnetic force of the periphery' [3: 463].

Peripheral resistance and disorder were provoked by a divided, unevenly developing Europe which was pushing outwards into a periphery viewed by metropolitan citizens with all the economic or political uncertainty, competitiveness, and other intellectual or cultural baggage considered in previous sections. It should be a truism, but it still seems to need emphasis, that peripheral conditions while no less are also no more important than those of Europe to an understanding of the imperialist drive. 'Peripheral' approaches to the problems of explanation are not simply to be substituted for somehow outdated or inadequate 'Eurocentric' ones. Certainly the stimulus to European contact and later imperial involvement often came from non-European initiatives or successful adaptation and rapid local change. Nevertheless, as the striking discontinuities in European conditions in the late century either impinged on other marked continuities of circumstance in the non-European world or cut across indigenous changes, they also stimulated the desire to dominate and decisions to dictate the future.

# 5 Other Recent Approaches

One approach to our topic, representing almost the polar opposite of peripheral explanations, is that which sees it as yet another, albeit striking, episode in the steady creation of the modern world economy. Developing perspectives derived from Marx, A.G. Frank and Fernand Braudel, Immanuel Wallerstein has started from the proposition that imperialism is the essential servant of an expanding capitalism [294; 295; cf. 277; 279]. He has published three of the four volumes intended to link historical fact with his theoretical argument, and his ideas are clear. Imperialism represents part of an inexorable process of incorporation by which the European capitalist 'core' of the world economy, needing to expand in response to internal pressures, gradually draws areas hitherto wholly external to it into a 'peripheral' or still closer 'semi-peripheral' position. This process, which has gathered momentum since the late fifteenth century, is portrayed as one of deepening capitalist development in the areas being linked in a global economic hierarchy to the highly developed core. Its outstanding features include the redirection of major trades, their replacement with new trades in primary products or raw materials required by the core, the transformation of production processes and global divisions of labour, and the enlargement of state structures, not least in the form of Europe's colonial empires, to organise the expanding economy.

Wallerstein's work has generated both enthusiasm for its scope and style, and, chiefly among historians, much criticism for its handling of evidence. Theory often appears to dominate and override awkward or ambiguous fact. His argument is highly deterministic and seems to have no place for causes or motives not purely economic. Distinctions between formal and informal empire, the nature and extent of political influence or control, the degree to which a European presence or influence had become unwelcome or oppressive, and variations in the imperialisms of different 'core' states, are all largely insignificant in this vision of modern world history. Equally problematical and anachronistic, given the acceptance by historians of European expansion of the vital role played by societies at the periphery, is Wallerstein's remarkable Eurocentrism. There is ample reason to think that forms of mercantile and manufacturing capitalism did not originate and develop simply in Europe, but were emerging in different societies – for example in India, Indonesia and parts of Africa – simultaneously from *c.* 1500 onwards. The engagement and interaction of these separate self-sustaining centres is a process quite distinct from mere incorporation by a European core [40; 222; 225; 247; 253; 281].

Nevertheless, the continuing popularity of such a 'world systems' approach is just one indicator of historians' resistance to the fragmentation of approaches and subject matter associated with 'peripheral' perspectives and the trend towards increasingly specialised scholarship among academics. In recent years there has consequently been a noticeable flight back to the metropole and a return to examination of both the domestic roots of European imperialism and its economic dimensions.

Studies, whether of diplomacy and international relations or of capitalist economics in relation to imperialism, have often focused on the impetus given to the process by the needs and calculations of the 'great powers', not least Germany, Britain and the United States, with their industrial and naval rivalry [6; 93; 94; 96; 97; 275: *chs 7–8*]. A case has been presented, however, for considering as a group the poorer, less developed powers – Italy, Portugal, Spain, possibly France and Russia – all with their larger landowners and large peasant populations still forming a substantial barrier to the development of urban, industrial and capitalist interests. Hit by serious agricultural malaise in the 'Great Depression' after 1870, possessing limited internal markets, uncompetitive yet desperately needing to export both agricultural produce and manufactures, these countries not only had an interest in imperialism but saw particular national advantages in territorial partitions to create protected colonies from which economically more powerful rivals would be excluded [31–33; 262]. Stronger powers, preferring free trade, were left with no choice but to compete for colonies and spheres of influence if their access to large parts of the globe was to be defended.

This hypothesis naturally provokes questions. Can these less-developed states justifiably be grouped together to include both Russia and France but to exclude Germany? Recent illuminating studies of the connections between French diplomacy and overseas economic expansion suggest not: they have emphasised the emergence of a close relationship between the state, officials and economic interests by the late 1890s, but one .geared to export industry and finance in a context of international cooperation or open competition, not one of exclusive French territorial possession [17; 183]. Is the suggestion of a substantial peasant interest in colonial expansion sustainable? Again this seems doubtful. As peasant export markets colonies were rarely significant. While some German and Italian politicians briefly looked to Africa as an outlet for emigration, emigrants themselves never took it seriously and made above all for the USA. The chronology and forms of protectionist pressures and measures within the states concerned have yet to be carefully juxtaposed with the imperial initiatives of all the powers, in order to establish the common patterns of socio-economic alliance and their real political impact both at home and overseas. It is known that rival powers' preference for 'free trade' was also far less neutral than the term itself might suggest; by maximising their existing advantages its practical effect was often protective in the same way as tariffs [8; 303: *ch. 6*]. Even without the presence of weaker, protectionist powers in Europe, it is far from clear that indigenous political and economic frameworks at the periphery could have continued to satisfy European demand without provoking annexation.

Nevertheless, the argument represents an imaginative attempt to restore a Marxist perspective to the analysis of late nineteenth-century imperialism. In a neat reversal of current thinking it applies the 'peripheral' outlook to Europe itself, portraying the initiative of the marginalised regions as critical in compelling the stronger powers to action. It addresses more effectively than Wallerstein's model of core, semi-periphery and periphery particular characteristics of both the period and the local societies with which we are concerned. It avoids a lop-sided emphasis on finance and capital exports, and once more tackles directly questions as to the manner in which the general needs of a capitalist system, experiencing ever more intense social and economic competition, might temporarily be met by the accumulation of new areas of operation.

Reflection on the distinctions to be drawn between types of European capitalist economy has also moved in another direction, with significant work focused on Britain's experience. Much research by economic and social historians in the last twenty years has questioned the vigour and scope of Britain's industrial revolution, has explored the continuing strength of commercial and financial interests in British life, and has revealed plenty about the workings of great centres like the City of London. These insights have provided the basis for Cain and Hopkins's attempt to redefine the nature of Britain's political economy as one of 'gentlemanly capitalism', a system forged during the eighteenth century in which 'an alliance . . . between the City, southern investors and the landed interest' came 'to play a leading role in Britain's overseas expansion until well into the twentieth century' [256: 469]. Developed in articles over more than a decade, and with added inspiration from a reconsideration of ideas found in J.A. Hobson's writings, their interpretation has been further elaborated in a major book just published [257–259].

For the later nineteenth century its implications are several and also highly contentious. Striking episodes such as Britain's occupation of Egypt and the South African War (1899–1902) are presented as originating in gentlemanly capitalists' needs for protection of their financial and commercial interests, and in their influence over government policy-making. Not only does the decade c.1870 lose any significance as a divide, but Cain and Hopkins insist on the fundamental continuity of metropolitan overseas expansion since well before 1750. We are thus faced with the reintegration on the domestic front of metropolitan economic needs, national government policy and formal as well as informal empire-building. More broadly still, in redefining a 'national' capitalism, the tendency of this analysis is to distance Britain from her continental neighbours, and to highlight the significance of local variations within any wider European capitalist framework. Already this work has generated considerable dissent, among historians of British society and politics as well as British trade and imperialism; the term is passing into common usage, and a sustained debate seems likely [149; 265; 284; 285].

Even if historians of other countries should follow this clear lead and explore further the relation of their own national economies and social elites to imperial ambitions, there seems little likelihood that the gentlemanly capitalist model can be successfully applied elsewhere [167; 183; 217]. However, fresh analysis with financial considerations in view may bear fruit in other ways. Again, the richness of British sources and breadth of Britain's overseas involvement have prompted a review of the late nineteenth century in order to address the questions: Who gained and who lost from empire? What were the financial costs and benefits of imperialism? [266].

Calculating the overall profit and loss of an imperial system undoubtedly poses interesting and very challenging questions, to which there are clearly no easy answers [272; 276; 280; 283]. Sources apart, both reaching agreement on what to assess and defining the cost implications of hypothetical alternatives to empire make this kind of national accounting a difficult art at the best of times.

Its relevance here arises from the light its findings may shed on the motives giving imperialism much of its impetus. Those consciously anticipating gains or actually profiting from imperial expansion are likely to support it. Following Hobson's logic, historians have often been tempted to say that to pinpoint the profiteer is to reveal the motor of imperialism, the principal source of imperial dynamism. Thus Huttenback and Davis's interesting work on taxation and business records has defined more precisely than before certain elite minority groups apparently gaining from empire, a finding which

Hopkins feels confirms the dominant influence he and Cain wish to associate with the City of London and southern investors [266:*chs 3, 7–8*; 272]. However, historians cannot remind themselves too often that an 'interest' like a 'presence' neither necessarily produces 'imperialism' nor indicates conclusively a significant functional contribution to imperial expansion, however formal or informal. Those connections always need to be explicitly demonstrated. Too often generalisations provide a flimsy covering for connections which are really no more than loosely circumstantial.

All of the works just mentioned, but most explicitly that of Cain and Hopkins, involve us yet again in discussion of the relation between imperialism and culture. Whether capitalism is or is not a form of economic activity inevitably generating an 'imperialist' culture at home and abroad is an old and still hotly debated issue. The concept of 'gentlemanly capitalism', for example, does not refer just to certain economic institutions. It encapsulates a society in which not only economic interest but certain beliefs, social habits, status and political connections outweighed all others, both at home and abroad, in shaping both general long-term expansion and the pattern of imperialism – British intervention and control – overseas.

Historians interested in the extent to which the processes of imperialism shaped metropolitan culture and vice versa, have recently been devoting attention to ways in which empire was deepened and sustained. Certain aspects of this have a long pedigree in studies of Europe's administrators, not only Britain's but more recently those of France, Belgium and Germany [263; 267–269; 271; 282]. Now this question is being tackled in new work on empire and sexuality, law enforcement and policing, and in some of the burgeoning literature on women and gender [250; 252; 254; 255; 260; 261; 293]. Examination of European, and notably British, involvement with hunting and the practice or policies of conservation has also contributed to our understanding of how western ways could undermine or alter non-European environments, preparing the way either for an initial colonisation or for the intensifying of colonial administrative intervention [101; 249; 270; 286; 309].

Recent studies of high culture in all its forms – the natural sciences, social sciences like anthropology, and scholarship in the humanities – have also made extensive claims for the power of European ideas to facilitate the subordination and control of the non-European world. For example, a study of the British geologist Sir Roderick Murchison concluded from his career that: 'Science has never been value-neutral or wholly objective; especially in the context of empire, it implies control, as an instrument both of administration and of knowledge . . . . The related disciplines of geology and geography exemplify the "subimperialism" of scientists – their desire for new data, careers, classificatory conquests, and power in administrative affairs – meshing with the needs of government' [291: 233]. European classifications and categories in biological and ethnographical studies as well as the conventions of cartography had been steadily extended since the sixteenth and especially eighteenth centuries [286]. To Europeans themselves, it is said, this knowledge brought power and control over the world around them, as well as prestige in the eyes of neighbouring rivals, confirmation of their role as agents of 'civilisation', and a measure of legitimacy in the eyes of extra-European people. Scholarship, it is argued, was often promoted by Europe's governments as well as individuals with these explicit aims [287; 308].

The extent to which intellectual, academic 'knowledge' brought authority and confidence, extended Europe's sense of the possible, and gave rise to alliances of convenience between scholars or experts and those with political and economic power, raises important questions. For some time anthropologists have agonised over the contribution made by their discipline to imperialism and the effectiveness of colonial rule. Misgivings arose over its tendency to define institutions and their functions, like those of chieftaincy or customary law, in ways which subtly denigrated them, deprived them of their natural flexibility, and restricted their capacity to adapt to the western impact [251; 264; 288; 290; 292]. Their professional debate, however, has been greatly extended by the influential work of Edward Said [289]. His interpretation of Europe's development of 'Orientalism' allots to this field of study (a phrase he deplores) a vital part in the delivery of the Near and Middle East to a western domination reaching far beyond formal political control. In place of Wallerstein's world economy, he offers incorporation into a no less oppressive global intellectual framework. The orientalists' studies were not simply misinterpreted and misused by the inexpert or ill-disposed. Far from giving rise to humane learning and sympathetic understanding, they themselves promoted caricatures and stereotypes; these shaped perceptions on all sides, non-Europeans absorbed them in their turn, and without them the extension of European influence and controls, the transformation of expansion into imperialism, would have been inconceivable. Far from providing accurate representations, knowledge of extra-European societies was warped by the purposes it was to serve.

Said's arguments are not only highly controversial but have profound implications both for the study of imperialism in all periods and for the modern relations of the west with the entire non-European world. These arise from his insistence that prevailing modes of western scholarship cannot achieve, and are not ultimately interested in, anything but a self-serving and therefore limited understanding of other alien societies. In defining Orientalism – 'a Western style for dominating, restructuring, and having authority over the Orient' – Said emphasises his debt to the ideas of western thinkers, such as Foucault, Gramsci and Raymond Williams, on the social conditioning of knowledge. His argument also has its parallels, however, with those non-European critics of imperialism, such as Fanon, who attach prime importance not to the economics of imperialism but to the cultural traits which made oppression both possible and acceptable, and proceed to stress the dehumanisation of both imperialists and their subjects.

Said focused chiefly on the Near and Middle East, and some have followed him there [278]. It is also possible to trace persistent images and representations in the writing of India's history by Europeans to support his broad interpretation [273; 274]. There are, however, good grounds for wariness of arguments which present these images of non-European societies either as conceived with superiority and domination in mind or as imposed figments of a purely European imagination. The literary bias of these analyses towards written texts, for example, leads them to underestimate or even to misunderstand entirely the circumstances in which texts were conceived or written. In particular, the common assumption that consciously or unconsciously the really influential or decisive context for the authors was that of expanding imperial power, encourages one to ignore the fact that Europe's own domestic problems or their own individual fantasies were often uppermost in the writers' minds [cf. 106]. Many 'orientalist' images, categories, for example, like those of 'caste' or 'martial races', also owed much to representations already commonly applied within the local societies concerned; they therefore possessed a value independent of European conceptions, and raise many questions about the conditioning of European knowledge by prior non-European ideas.

Some historians, influenced not only by Said but by linguistic analysis of the relation which both language and written texts have to their social setting, have been attracted to the concept of 'colonial' or 'imperial discourse'. By this they mean the existence at a particular time of a specific terminology, discernible patterns of linguistic usage, and underlying logical or conceptual assumptions, combined in the discussion of imperial issues with the clear purpose of exercising power and control over other peoples. The study of imperial culture along these lines is in its infancy, and its value still uncertain. Although the idea of a 'colonial discourse' implies a marked specialisation in both the context and the use of vocabulary, it is perhaps difficult to reconcile such a degree of definition with the reality of everyday communication. It seems to neglect the extent to which language is constantly in a state of flux, as well as the different starting points – for instance, generation, upbringing and education – of participants in the exchanges. In order to illustrate the difficulty of deciding whether a state of definition and common agreement sufficient to merit the term 'discourse' had been achieved, it is only necessary to consider the shifting and varied use of certain key words such as 'native', 'primitive', 'slavery' or 'race'. While the language of small and carefully selected groups, such as French officials handling colonial affairs in the 1890s, may be pleasingly coherent, there are limits to what it can tell us about the wider society, especially if one is trying to think comparatively in European terms. The concept of a 'discourse' is itself extremely slippery. It is liable to move uneasily between a language in general use which comes to be applied to a specific subject, and the language specifically generated by a subject which dictates the use of certain terms as points of reference. The language of European missionaries, for example, about Christianity and conversion is full of such ambiguities.

In terms therefore of what actually happened, it is far more difficult to link collected texts and literary or linguistic traditions with imperialist outcomes than today's critics of the nineteenth century's contemporary 'orientalists' allow.

# 6 Expansion and Empire

Underlying this discussion has been an attempt to distinguish between the broad expansion of Europe and the more limited but growing phenomenon of domination or actual control of people and their territory by individual European powers. I have argued that those conditions which made for European expansion did not necessarily produce imperial consequences. When expansion manifested itself in the shape of informal or formal empire, when interest, influence or ambition were converted into control, that transformation can only be understood and explained by analysis of the politics, economy and society of both the European and extra-European parties involved in each particular case.

Not all European powers were equally interested in converting expansion into empire, and the success of those who were varied greatly. The Dutch were too small to attempt it on any significant scale, the Portuguese too weak to do more than try to exploit what they already held. The British were anxious to avoid adding control and further direct responsibilities to their existing commitments, and expressed their 'imperial' ambitions above all in support for the more intensive development of existing formal possessions like India and the Dominions. Germany and Italy, however, went to considerable lengths to acquire the substance of empire. Their success was limited. Italy's gains depended on the tolerance and self-denial of others, and Germany's expansiveness, expressed after 1895 in terms which alarmed too many potential rivals, was not turned to significant imperial account.

Particularly striking is the way in which the accidents or opportunities shaping Europe's presence overseas before 1860 continued to exert their influence on later expansion. A glance at the areas of British trade and missionary activity which had clearly emerged by the 1850s in Sierra Leone, the Gold Coast and (as it later became) southern Nigeria, shows that they were not simply footholds for further advances, but remained the permanent core of Britain's influence and later territorial empire in West Africa. In similar fashion, the long-standing French missionary and commercial interest in Indo-China provided the basis for armed interventions and successive conquests of territory, supported either from Paris by Napoleon III in the 1860s and Jules Ferry two decades later, or by local officials, Admiral Dupré and Francis Garnier in the early 1870s, Admiral Courbet and Henri Rivière in 1882-3.

In both West Africa and mainland South-East Asia, the early arrivals, Britain and France, dominated the regional partitions which took place after 1860 to the virtual exclusion of other European powers. Late-comers on the scene – either as nation states out to assert their international presence, or as major commercial and industrial countries – if they wanted territory were left to compete for the relatively worthless or utterly insignificant remains. Thus Germany was allowed to acquire South-West Africa, Tanganyika and a selection of Pacific islands, and Italy pursued its ambitions in some of the more dessicated parts of Africa.

These variations between states thus depended on many factors, such as size, resources, domestic politics, timing and opportunity. Within each European country, officials or politicians frequently differed amongst themselves and from sections of their own people. The conditions of the extra-European world were quite as fluid and no less diverse. Non-Europeans often welcomed aspects of Europe's expansion as powerful aids to their own prosperity and aggrandisement. In these circumstances, the accidental and unpredictable played an important role, and at least in the early part of our period there remained plenty of scope for adjustment and compromise by all parties in pursuit of their interests.

One of the principal strands in the process by which imperialism came to assume much greater importance lay in the European political revolution achieved by Germany's emergence from the wars of 1866 and 1870, French defeat and the establishment of the Third Republic, the humbling of Austria and the unification of Italy, and Russia's reassertion of her position. The combination of sentimental nationalisms and diplomatic manoeuvring thus unleashed remained a persistently disruptive and aggravating force. The instability it caused was only worsened by the failure of any obviously dominant power or combination of powers to emerge. Countries such as Britain, Portugal and Belgium found themselves by steps drawn inexorably into the jockeying for position. As the diplomatic, strategic and possibly material potential of new areas outside Europe became evident, metropolitan governments moved to exploit it, some eventually clutching at almost any issue which held out hope of tipping the European balance in their own favour. Tunisia, Egypt, South Africa, Morocco and Persia, as well as Chinese territory were all used in this way between 1880 and 1914.

The upheavals of the 1860s were also in a distinct sense economic, as the expansive enthusiasms characteristic of the early part of the decade ran their course in a global environment seriously complicated by the impact of wars on levels of production, international competition, national debts and rearmament. Economic fluctuations and uncertainties were in consequence real enough for twenty-five years after 1870 and cast a still longer shadow. While not the universal and unrelievedly gloomy Great Depression of some contemporary descriptions, they caused periodic and widespread disquiet. Politicians everywhere came under pressure to assist the canny, the fearful and the afflicted among their electorates. The timing and extent of their responses varied from country to country, but one by one different national governments showed themselves more willing to act in defence of their citizens' economic well-being than they had been at the beginning of our period. Apart from Britain and, to a lesser degree, Germany, few resisted after the mid-1870s the turn to all manner of protective devices and resort to retaliation. For every European state, especially between 1880 and 1900, not only protectorates and formalised spheres of influence but ever more direct colonial control became a useful weapon in the domestic political and economic armoury as well as the diplomatic one.

Of course these two armouries could not be kept separate. Diplomatic horsetrading with European counterparts carried little conviction if the horses had no flesh on them, as the British found to their cost in relations with the French in West Africa. When the Anglo-French boundary agreements of 1890–1 involving the Niger territories were found to rest on inflated claims about British trade and treaties, the French fought to have them revised. Similarly, diplomatic influence with South American, Ottoman, Persian or Chinese governments was non-existent, and national interests of any kind therefore perceived as barely protected, unless underpinned with European cash or assistance in some tangible form. In these parts of the world, where indigenous or local governments retained some resilience and a relatively independent existence despite their weaknesses, older and newer imperial powers competed on a more equal footing. There European governments were increasingly disposed after 1880 to counter the possibility of damaging rival influences by lending their official backing to unofficial enterprise. Thus Britain, fearful of Germany and Russia, officially supported the private ambitions of English bankers and concessionaires in Turkey or Persia. Her diplomats vied with those of France and Germany in lobbying at Peking with promises of the benefits to China from European loans and grants of railway concessions.

Technological change made for European vulnerability as well as strength, and was rapidly increasing the importance of access to extra-European territory. For the Great Powers global trading networks had to be defended in case of war; coaling stations, telegraph cables, dry docks and ever more sophisticated port facilities were required in peacetime. The ability to be able to rely constantly on local authorities thus assumed greater importance for more Europeans than ever before. At the same time not only was Europeans' confidence in that reliability being undermined by growing familiarity and experience, but non-Europeans themselves moved in contrary directions to secure their own interests in the face of more intrusive official or unofficial European demands or expectations. China's resistance to western penetration had long been legendary. However, despite previous setbacks in

1842 and 1860 when they had been forced to open the so-called 'Treaty Ports' to European trade, the Chinese again tried to stem the tide after 1880. They reasserted their historic claims by declaring a protectorate over Tonkin in 1881, and fought in support of the Vietnamese against the French invaders until the peace treaty of Tientsin in June 1885. Inside China, at a more popular level but often with official encouragement, anti-foreign demonstrations became increasingly common. Past achievements and future possibilities for expansion at home and abroad thus required protection; to guarantee that protection imperialism often seemed inescapable and even desirable.

In recent years, as this essay has tried to demonstrate, the work on imperialism of French, Dutch, British and German scholars has slowly become more accessible even to those in each country without a foreign language. Although the work of British and German historians in particular has influenced the shape of much current research and debate, there nevertheless can hardly be said to exist a common set of concerns, let alone a dominant interpretation of the relations between expansion and 'imperialism'. My survey of debates and controversies has therefore necessarily drawn attention to widely contrasting approaches, and has illustrated some of the difficulties to be encountered in reaching agreement over these highly complex issues. I have tried to indicate the limited areas to which existing theories may apply, and to raise significant questions about fashions in historical enquiry.

This approach, of course, is not the only one which could have been chosen. Some readers, thinking it far easier to ask questions than to provide answers, and less difficult to criticise generalisations than to provide them in the first place, may find it insufficiently constructive for their tastes. However, I hope that they will be prepared to agree that it is not altogether inappropriate. Judging from the careless confidence with which pronouncements are often made about 'imperialism', a little more caution, a few more obvious preliminary questions, even perhaps a greater humility in the face of the limits to historical explanation, are unlikely to be misplaced in this field. Nothing written above is intended to suggest that historical study should be confined to the accumulation of facts at the expense of developing our understanding. Narrative synthesis and generalisation are essential tasks for any historian, because without them there can be no comprehension of the past.

In our attempts to understand the transformations of European expansion and the 'imperialism' of the period 1860 to 1914, appeals, for example, to particular forms of capitalism, to metropolitan diplomatic or social dynamics, to cultural incompatibility or economic conflict between European and non-European societies, nevertheless take us only part of the way. Often taken individually to provide general explanations, even if not offered as such, they too easily obscure the essential conjunctures of contrasting conditions which characterise these years.

Historians examining the 'economic foundations' of expansion overseas may reasonably conclude that 'this widening interest in imperialism was a function of the spread of industrialisation in Europe, especially after 1870' [10: 67]. Such a judgement would not now be regarded as unduly risqué or adventurous, for it leaves open for consideration both what might be involved in the 'functional' nature of imperialism, and the economic variety covered by the term industrialisation. It would be quite another thing, however, as well as deeply questionable, to argue that the foundations of expansion overseas were essentially economic, or that the economic dimension to extensions of European control and influence was always in the end the determining factor.

Such formulations are constantly undermined by the behaviour of different imperial powers. The shifting nature of successive German governments' interest in the Samoan islands is especially marked [175]. In the late 1870s and early 1880s European economic rivalries did not result in annexation; only in the wider context created by the Spanish-American War of 1898, international crisis in China, Britain's interest in settling a range of irritating colonial boundary disputes, and Germany's domestic political difficulties, was it found desirable to agree on a colonial partition in November 1899. Even then, the USA, Britain and Germany were content to maintain open international trade. In other settings, the behaviour of Britain and Germany as compared with that of

France and Portugal clearly demonstrates that protective tariffs were tied chiefly to particular forms of nationalism rather than with 'capitalism' or 'industrialisation' *per se*.

In case after case economic interest is found either to be inseparably linked with other motives or was something cited by contemporaries in search of rational justifications for policies and practices which originated with quite other and more potent preoccupations. While this makes general explanatory accounts or satisfying theories of European expansion and imperialism the more difficult to provide, it usefully emphasises the basic requirement that they should bring out the interlocking character of many different spheres of contemporary life. While tacitly acknowledging the need for wider perspectives, existing accounts nevertheless rarely offer more than brief genuflections towards, for example, 'social darwinist' ideas or the Maxim gun.

The kind of interconnections which students of imperialism need to be able to make can perhaps be illustrated by a brief general reference to the technology of the age. The persistent application of mechanical inventiveness to industrial processes had not only made possible the expansion of European manufacturing output and with it the need for wider markets; it had also swelled demand for many raw materials, such as tin, rubber or copper, so widening Europe's need for industrial supplies. Advances in communication – railways, steam shipping and telegraphs – were the product of that same technical ingenuity, and contributed along with developments in commercial and financial management to the ease with which wider markets could be served or the most distant commodities be exploited. Medical advances and, perhaps still more, the increasingly careful organisation of urban living, made possible the greater likelihood of expatriates' survival and management of overseas concerns. As a last resort, the growing power of European weaponry, and the improved ability to deploy armed forces, meant that markets, supplies, communications and installations could be more easily safeguarded or conquered in the face of local or international hostility. Technological change thus helped not only to integrate the world economy, but contributed to the economic slumps of the later nineteenth century for which imperial activity was sometimes perceived as a cure, and made more practicable both that imperialism and the projection of European influence. A very pronounced shift of the technological balance of power thus took place after 1860 in favour of the European world. Yet it would be no more persuasive to argue that European expansion was above all technologically determined than that it was economically driven.

Perceptions of economic opportunity and choices as to which openings were exploited are inseparable from mental habits and ethical frameworks of thought. The connection of technology and imperialism is no less bound up with conceptual and institutional considerations, shaped not only in this period by such influences as religion, religious doubt, or views of the right relationship between individual and state. Technology was, for instance, directly related to the violence or threat of violence which figured so considerably in the extension of European influence and territorial control before 1914. That this was so depended not on the mere existence of a technological gap or even of advanced weapons themselves, but on the decisions to use them [321].

These decisions were naturally affected by many factors. Some were in a way trivial. Force used against slave traders was not only widely acceptable but highly commended, even if not always in practice what it claimed to be. As one disillusioned recruit wrote home from central Africa in 1895: 'It is a considerable farce this slave freeing business. In the first place I've no doubt that a great many of the so-called slaves are not slaves at all. But like the mission converts, freed slaves pay well at home. People get K.C.M.G's and C.M.G's and so on for freeing slaves' [74: *299 n.21*]. But distance could lend enchantment, and metropolitan detachment from or obliviousness to the reality or even occurrence of colonial wars and retribution enabled atrocities to go unchecked and comfortable assumptions about civilising missions to persist. Far more often, however, violence neither acquired nor was felt to need disguise. Technology was applied to the enforcement of European wishes or rule, and those few who argued that political ingenuity, economic flexibility and Europe's own technical resources made imperialism avoidable and unnecessary were brushed aside [56]. This resulted ultimately from the pervasive metroplitan *mentalités* which combined in their varied ways increasingly strident nationalism with concepts of race and the growing insistence on cultural superiority.

As the British showed in their dealings with the Transvaal's Afrikaners at the time of the South African War (1899–1902), these assumptions could have disastrous consequences even for people of European origin. Elsewhere Russian and German activity provided comparable examples. Some extra-European societies themselves generated a similarly virulent exclusiveness. That this did not result simply from the adoption of European categories is clear both from China's treatment of her minority peoples and other 'barbarians', and (despite obvious parallels with the West's imperialism) from Japan's expansion into Korea and Formosa (Taiwan) after the Sino-Japanese War of 1894–5 [143; 296; 319].

It is in illuminating such areas that the recent work by historians of Europe's imperial cultures will ultimately prove of great value, especially as recent British work comes to be joined by that of continental scholars. Fuller knowledge and understanding of the manner in which metropolitan *mentalités* shaped the processes of empire-building, of ways in which appeals to empire and imperial activity came to confer legitimacy and emerged as an important or persuasive rhetorical device for interests of many kinds, is needed at least to balance that which already exists of diplomacy, politics and economic interest. It is to be hoped that the parallel history of extra-European societies will also continue to be unravelled. The extent to which European ideas and techniques were appropriated, adapted and newly employed, is still imperfectly understood. Such comparative studies will eventually provide a far better basis than is available to historians at present for tackling that great intellectual challenge, the provision of a genuinely comprehensive analysis of Europe's late nineteenth-century imperialism.

# Select Bibliography

This provides suggestions for further reading of several kinds. It includes introductory surveys both to Europe as a whole and to the imperialism of individual states. A number of items falling outside the years 1860–1914 it is hoped will emphasise the historical continuity of the issues being discussed. Accessibility, as well as topicality, intrinsic interest and relative importance, has been an important consideration in making the selection, although unfortunately not all items are easily obtainable.

## Abbreviations

| | |
|---|---|
| *EcHR* | *Economic History Review* |
| *HJ* | *Historical Journal* |
| *JAH* | *Journal of African History* |
| *JICH* | *Journal of Imperial and Commonwealth History* |
| *MAS* | *Modern Asian Studies* |
| *P&P* | *Past and Present* |
| *RFHOM* | *Revue Française de l'Histoire d'Outre Mer* |
| *TRHS* | *Transactions of the Royal Historical Society* |

## General Surveys

[1] R. Betts, *The False Dawn: European Imperialism in the Nineteenth Century* (Oxford/Minneapolis, 1976).

[2] Phillip Darby, *Three Faces of Imperialism: British and American Approaches to Asia and Africa 1870–1970* (New Haven/London, 1987).

[3] D.K. Fieldhouse, *Economics and Empire 1830–1914* (London, 1973; rep. 1984): exhaustive study of main European powers, whose imperialism represents a political response to instability in areas of European interest.

[4] D.K. Fieldhouse, *The Colonial Empires: a Comparative Survey from the Eighteenth Century* (London, 1966; rep. 1982).

[5] E.J. Hobsbawm, *The Age of Empire, 1870–1914* (London, 1987): notable for its range of reference and metropolitan sense of period, rather than its insight into empire-building.

[6] Paul Kennedy, *The Rise and Fall of the Great Powers: Economic Change and Military Conflict from 1500 to 2000* (New York, 1987; London, 1988).

[7] V.G. Kiernan, *European Empires from Conquest to Collapse, 1815–1960* (London, 1982): focuses on war and imperialism, with a wealth of comparative detail.

[8] Tony Smith, *The Pattern of Imperialism: the United States, Great Britain and the Late-industrializing World since 1815* (Cambridge, 1981): considers the replacement of British by American hegemony since *c.* 1890.

## Belgium

[9] J. Stengers, 'King Leopold's Imperialism', in [317] pp. 248–75: a valuable, wide-ranging essay by the master of a subject on aspects of which there are many exceptionally detailed studies.

## Britain

[10] P.J. Cain, *Economic Foundations of British Overseas Expansion 1815–1914* (London, 1980): surveys the extensive literature, arguing for integration of persistent metropolitan economic needs into any explanation.

[11] Ronald Hyam, *Britain's Imperial Century 1815–1914: A Study of Empire and Expansion* (London, 1976; 2nd edn, forthcoming): stimulating analysis of the relationship between formal and informal empire within the framework of Britain's global expansion.

[12] A.N. Porter, *An Atlas of British Overseas Expansion* (London, 1991): useful reference, maps plus commentary.

[13] Bernard Porter, *The Lion's Share: A Short History of British Imperialism 1850–1970* (1975; 2nd edn, 1984): attractive presentation of case for late nineteenth-century expansion as evidence and source of Britain's weakness, contrary to many contemporary expectations.

## France

[14] C.M. Andrew and A.S. Kanya-Forstner, *France Overseas. The Great War and the Climax of French Imperial Expansion* (London, 1981).

[15] H. Brunschwig, *The Myth of French Imperialism 1870–1914* (London, 1961): influential account of French expansion in search of prestige and national self-confidence.

[16] R. Girardet, *L'idée coloniale en France 1871–1962* (Paris, 1972): very useful survey of the many French ideas about empire.

[17] Jacques Thobie, *La France impériale 1880–1914* (Paris, 1982): impressive analysis of French imperialism as a developing form of 'finance capitalism'.

## Germany

[18] W.O. Henderson, *Studies in German Colonial History* (London, 1962): contains useful essays on the period before 1914, including German economic penetration into the Middle East.

[19] Woodruff D. Smith, *The German Colonial Empire* (Chapel Hill, NC, 1978): a very useful introductory survey.

*Italy*

[20] J.-L. Miège, *L'Impérialisme colonial italien de 1870 à nos jours* (Paris, 1968): argues for Italian imperialism as a case of ancient traditions revived in the context of a new national unity, strongly ideological not economic in content.

*Netherlands*

[21] M. Kuitenbrouwer, *The Netherlands and the Rise of Modern Imperialism: Colonies and Foreign Policy 1870–1902*, trans. H. Beyer (1985; Oxford, 1991): using British, Portuguese and Belgian comparisons, argues forcefully that the Dutch participated fully in the imperialism of the age.

[22] J.T. Lindblad, 'Economic Aspects of the Dutch Expansion in Indonesia, 1870–1914', *MAS*, 23 (1989), 1–23.

[23] H.L. Wesseling, 'The Netherlands and the Partition of Africa', *JAH*, 22 (1981), 495–509: argues that the Dutch were not simply bystanders, even if diplomatically uninvolved.

[24] H.L. Wesseling, 'The Giant that was a Dwarf, or the Strange History of Dutch Imperialism', *JICH*, XVI, 3 (1988), 58–70: addresses the problems of conceptualising a Dutch late nineteenth-century 'imperialism'.

*Portugal*

[25] Gervase Clarence-Smith, *The Third Portuguese Empire 1825–1975: A Study in Economic Imperialism* (Manchester, 1985): argues powerfully against the views of [26] that the Portuguese were intent simply on prestige, national status and revival of past glories. See also [33].

[26] R.J. Hammond, *Portugal and Africa 1815–1910: A Study in Uneconomic Imperialism* (Stanford, 1966).

*Russia*

[27] Dietrich Geyer, *Russian Imperialism: The Interaction of Domestic and Foreign Policy 1860–1914* (trans. Bruce Little) (Gottingen, 1977; Leamington Spa, 1987): the only connected and impressive account in English of its subject.

[28] Taras Hunczak (ed.), *Russian Imperialism from Ivan the Great to the Revolution* (New Brunswick, NJ, 1974): like [29], a useful collection of separate studies, stressing the continuity of Russian expansion.

[29] Michael Rwykin (ed.), *Russian Colonial Expansion to 1917* (London, New York, 1988).

*Spain*

[30] Raymond Carr, *Spain, 1808–1975* (2nd edn, Oxford, 1982): provides informative details.

[31] W.G. Clarence-Smith, 'The Economic Dynamics of Spanish Colonialism in the Nineteenth and Twentieth Centuries', *Itinerario*, 15 (1991), 71–90: with [32], an important demonstration of what empire meant economically to Spaniards at different periods.

[32] W.G. Clarence-Smith, 'The Economic Dynamics of Spanish Imperialism 1898–1945', in V. Morales Lezcano (ed.), *Il Aula Canarias y el Noroeste de Africa* (Las Palmas, 1988), pp. 17–28.

[33] Gervase Clarence-Smith, 'The Portuguese and Spanish roles in the Scramble for Africa: an economic interpretation', in [301] pp. 215–27: emphasises parallels between the two cases.


*After 1914*

[34] F. Ansprenger, *The Dissolution of the Colonial Empires* (London, 1989).

[35] Jean Bouvier, René Girault and Jacques Thobie, *L'Impérialisme à la française 1914–1960* (Paris, 1986).

[36] John Darwin, *Britain and Decolonisation: the Retreat from Empire in the Post-war World* (Basingstoke, 1988).

[37] R.F. Holland, *European Decolonization 1918–1981: an Introductory Survey* (Basingstoke, 1985).

[38] Jacques Marseille, *Empire colonial et capitalisme français: histoire d'un divorce* (Paris, 1984).

# 1   Definitions and Theories

[39] Winfried Baumgart, *Imperialism. The Idea and Reality of British and French Colonial Expansion, 1880–1914* (rev. edn, Oxford, 1982): with a narrow definition (acquisition of formal political control over territory) and focus (Africa), he has no difficulty in revealing drawbacks in theories including Wehler's 'social imperialism'.

[40] Anthony Brewer, *Marxist Theories of Imperialism. A Critical Survey* (2nd edn, London, 1990): also includes chapters on J.A. Hobson and others.

[41] Benjamin J. Cohen, *The Question of Imperialism. The Political Economy of Dominance and Dependence* (New York/London, 1974).

[42] Michael W. Doyle, *Empires* (Ithaca/London, 1986).

[43] Norman Etherington, 'The Capitalist Theory of Capitalist Imperialism', *History of Political Economy*, 15 (1983), 654–78: explores capitalist arguments c.1900 supporting imperialism as rational and necessary.

[44] Norman Etherington, *Theories of Imperialism. War, Conquest and Capital* (Beckenham, 1984): a valuable survey of theories as they have developed against the background of twentieth-century events, and a plea

for recognition of the distinctions between imperialism, colonialism, and the expansion of capitalism, in aid of effective explanation.

[45] D.K. Fieldhouse, *Colonialism 1870–1945. An Introduction* (London, 1981).

[46] John Gallagher and Ronald Robinson, 'The Imperialism of Free Trade', *EcHR*, 6 (1953), 1–15 (reprinted variously, and in [54]): immensely influential and justifiably famous essay which shifted attention from formal empire and its classic expression in Africa's colonial partition to the varied patterns of imperialism consequent on Britain's and Europe's global economic expansion.

[47] Michael Hechter, *Internal Colonialism. The Celtic Fringe in British National Development 1536–1966* (London, 1975): with [59], provides illustrations of 'imperialism' as an internal European phenomenon.

[48] J.A. Hobson, *Imperialism. A Study* (London, 1902).

[49] Thomas Hodgkin, 'Some African and Third World Theories of Imperialism', in [317] pp. 93–116.

[50] Paul Kennedy, 'Continuity and Discontinuity in British Imperialism 1815–1914' in [298] pp. 20–38.

[51] R. Koebner, *Empire* (Cambridge, 1961): see [52].

[52] R. Koebner and H.D. Schmidt, *Imperialism. The Story and Significance of a Political Word, 1840–1960* (Cambridge, 1964): with [51], provides important study of semantic roots and changing usage.

[53] V.I. Lenin, *Imperialism: The Highest Stage of Capitalism* [(1916) edition by Lawrence and Wishart, London, 1942].

[54] Wm Roger Louis, *Imperialism. The Robinson and Gallagher Controversy* (New York, 1976): usefully surveys the often confusing debate which followed from [46] and [239].

[55] Wolfgang J. Mommsen, *Theories of Imperialism* (London and New York, 1981): a usefully succinct, critical survey intended to provide a 'bridge between English and continental thought on the nature of imperialism'.

[56] Bernard Porter, *Critics of Empire. British Radical Attitudes to Colonialism in Africa 1895–1914* (London, 1968): pathbreaking and highly illuminating study of contemporary debates, important for Hobson, Mary Kingsley and E.D. Morel.

[57] Charles Reynolds, *Modes of Imperialism* (Oxford, 1981): useful discussion of the relationship between theory and effective explanation.

[58] J.A. Schumpeter, *Imperialism and Social Classes*, ed. and with Introduction by Paul M. Sweezy (Oxford, 1951).

[59] S. Sideri, *Trade and Power: Informal Colonialism in Anglo-Portuguese Relations* (Rotterdam, 1970): illustrates the difficulty of confining analyses of imperialism to the non-European world.

[60] Eric Stokes, 'Late Nineteenth-Century Colonial Expansion and the Attack on the Theory of Economic Imperialism: a case of mistaken identity?', *HJ*, 12 (1969), 285–301: pinpoints the important distinction drawn by Lenin, but missed by many of his subsequent critics, between colonial expansion before 1900 and imperialism thereafter, and comments on its significance for historians now.

[61] C.M. Andrew and A.S. Kanya-Forstner, 'Gabriel Hanotaux, the Colonial Party and the Fashoda Strategy', *JICH*, III (1974/5), 55–104; a fine illustration of the thesis argued in [62].

[62] C.M. Andrew and A.S. Kanya-Forstner, 'Centre and Periphery in the Making of the Second French Colonial Empire 1815–1920', *JICH*, XVI, 3 (1988), 9–34: colonial expansion followed from enthusiasts' ability to exploit 'the incoherence of official policy-making and the fervent nationalism of French society'.

[63] Roger Anstey, *The Atlantic Slave Trade and British Abolition, 1760–1810* (London, 1975).

[64] David Arnold (ed.), *Imperial Medicine and Indigenous Societies* (Manchester, 1988).

[65] T.G. August, *The Selling of the Empire: British and French Imperialist Propaganda 1890–1940* (Westport, Conn., 1985): may be usefully compared with [100] and [121].

[66] S. Avineri (ed.), *Karl Marx on Colonialism and Modernization* (New York, 1968): an extensive selection from Marx's writings.

[67] Eric Axelson, *Portugal and the Scramble for Africa 1875–1891* (Johannesburg, 1967): with [132], illustrates the difficulties of a weaker European player in the imperialist stakes.

[68] E.A. Ayandele, *The Missionary Impact on Modern Nigeria 1842–1914* (London, 1966): important study based largely on Protestant sources.

[69] Klaus J. Bade, 'Imperial Germany and West Africa: Colonial Movement, Business Interests, and Bismarck's "Colonial Policies"', in [301] pp. 121–47: taken with [82], [110] and [126], provides the best recent analysis of the varied interests influencing German colonial initiatives in the 1880s.

[70] V. Berghahn, *Militarism. The History of an International Debate 1861–1979* (Cambridge, 1984).

[71] Helmut Bley, *South West Africa under German Rule 1894–1914* (trans. H. Ridley, London, 1971): using German sources, reveals much about German attitudes and policy.

[72] Christine Bolt, *Victorian Attitudes to Race* (London, 1971): concentrates on the mid-century hardening of views, under the influence of developments in scientific thought and experience of colonial rule.

[73] Patrick Brantlinger, *Rule of Darkness. British Literature and Imperialism, 1830–1914* (Ithaca, 1988).

[74] H.A.C. Cairns, *Prelude to Imperialism. British Reactions to Central African Society 1840–1890* (London, 1965): an excellent, nuanced study of growing knowledge and changing perceptions.

[75] P.A. Cohen, 'Christian Missions and their Impact to 1900', in J.K. Fairbank (ed.), *The Cambridge History of China*, vol. 10 (Cambridge, 1978).

[76] W.B. Cohen, *The French Encounter with Africans: White Response to Blacks 1530–1880* (Bloomington, 1980): with [121], provides a useful introduction to French racial attitudes.

[77] David Brion Davis, *Slavery and Human Progress* (Oxford UP, 1984).

[78] Felix Driver, 'Henry Morton Stanley and his Critics: Geography, Exploration and Empire', *P&P*, 133 (1991), 134–66: exposes the debates for and against exploration or imperial penetration triggered off by Stanley's journeys and methods.

[79] G. Eley and D. Blackbourn, *The Peculiarities of German History: Bourgeois Society and Politics in Nineteenth-Century Germany* (Oxford, 1984).

[80] Geoff Eley, *From Unification to Nazism. Reinterpreting the German Past* (London and Boston (Mass.), 1986).

[81] Marc Gilbert, 'The Malda Incident: a Study in Imperial Diplomacy, Local Agency and Indian Nationalism', *JICH*, XIII (1985), 117–38: see [67], [86] and [132].

[82] Horst Grunder, 'Christian Missionary Activities in Africa in the Age of Imperialism and the Berlin Conference of 1884–1885', in [301] pp. 85–103: useful introduction to a wide range of missionary enterprise and its interplay with European government initiatives, in the 1870s and 1880s.

[83] John D. Hargreaves, *Prelude to the Partition of West Africa* (London, 1963): a fine study of growing European involvement and official diplomacy up to 1885.

[84] Freda Harcourt, 'Disraeli's Imperialism, 1866–1868: a Question of Timing', *HJ*, 23 (1980), 87–109: with [85], applies a 'social imperialist' analysis to the conventional watershed of 1870, and finds a common response in political leaders.

[85] Freda Harcourt, 'Gladstone, Monarchism and the "New" Imperialism, 1868–74', *JICH*, XIV (1985), 20–51.

[86] P.H.S. Hatton, 'Harcourt and Solf: the Search for an Anglo-German Understanding through Africa, 1912–14', *European Studies Review*, I (1971), 123–45: see also [67] and [132].

[87] Daniel R. Headrick, *The Tools of Empire: Technology and European Imperialism in the Nineteenth Century* (New York and Oxford, 1981): with [88], brings together details of advancing technologies available to empire-builders.

[88] Daniel R. Headrick, *The Tentacles of Progress. Technology Transfer in the Age of Imperialism, 1850–1940* (New York and Oxford, 1988).

[89] Michael Howard, 'Empire, Race and War in pre-1914 Britain', in Hugh Lloyd-Jones et al. (eds), *History and Imagination: Essays in Honour of H.R. Trevor-Roper* (London, 1981), pp. 340–55.

[90] R.C. Howell, *The Royal Navy and the Slave Trade* (Beckenham, 1987): see also [108, 109].

[91] Ronald Hyam, *Empire and Sexuality. The British Experience* (Manchester, 1990).

[92] A.S. Kanya-Forstner, *The Conquest of the Western Sudan. A Study in French Military Imperialism* (Cambridge, 1969): classic analysis of military expatriates' ability to get their way whatever the wishes of governments in Paris.

[93] Paul M. Kennedy, *The Rise of the Anglo-German Antagonism 1860–1914* (London, 1980): an impressive interweaving of politics, economics and foreign policy on a global scale.

[94] Paul M. Kennedy, *The Realities behind Diplomacy: Background Influences on British External Policy, 1865–1980* (London, 1981): from a metropolitan standpoint, sheds much light on the conditions affecting diplomatic manoeuvre.

[95] Paul M. Kennedy and A.J. Nicholls, *Nationalist and Racialist Movements in Britain and Germany before 1914* (1981): provides a good comparative introduction to a very wide field.

[96] William L. Langer, *The Diplomacy of Imperialism 1890–1902* (2nd edn, New York, 1951): with [97], traditional diplomatic history of the best kind.

[97] William L. Langer, *European Alliances and Alignments, 1871–1890* (2nd edn New York, 1950).

[98] D.A. Lorimer, *Colour, Class and the Victorians. English Attitudes to the Negro in the Mid-nineteenth Century* (Leicester UP, 1978): argues that the growth of racialism was 'as much a product of developments in the white world of England as a result of the multi-coloured world of the Empire'.

[99] C.J. Lowe, *Salisbury and the Mediterranean 1886–1896* (London, 1965).

[100] John M. MacKenzie, *Propaganda and Empire. The Manipulation of British Public Opinion 1880–1960* (Manchester, 1984): an influential study which rejects suggestions that the British were largely indifferent to imperialism, and explains why in reality imperial sentiment was so pervasive and persistent.

[101] John M. MacKenzie, *The Empire of Nature. Hunting, Conservation and British Imperialism* (Manchester, 1988).

[102] Roy Macleod and Milton Lewis (eds), *Disease, Medicine and Empire: Perspectives on Western Medicine and the Experience of European Expansion* (London, 1988).

[103] J.A. Mangan (ed.), *'Benefits Bestowed'? Education and British Imperialism* (Manchester, 1988).

[104] J.A. Mangan, *The Games Ethic and Imperialism* (London, 1986).

[105] J.A. Mangan, *Making Imperial Mentalities. Socialisation and British Imperialism* (Manchester, 1990): with [64], [100], [103] and [104] is one among a growing number of studies concerned to illustrate the many ways in which widespread acceptance and approval of a 'dominant imperial ideology' was promoted among both colonisers and colonised.

[106] P.J. Marshall and Glyndwr Williams, *The Great Map of Mankind: British Perceptions of the World in the Age of the Enlightenment* (London, 1982): the British intellectual world was not self-contained, and this throws much light on the growth of common European images or comparative judgements important to later imperial assertiveness.

[107] Gordon Martel, *Imperial Diplomacy: Rosebery and the Failure of Foreign Policy* (London and Kingston (Ont.), 1986).

[108] Suzanne Miers, *Britain and the Ending of the Slave Trade* (London, 1975): with [109], examines the relation of humanitarian commitment with other European motives for intervention in Africa.

85

[109] Suzanne Miers, 'Humanitarianism at Berlin: Myth or Reality?', in [301] pp. 333–45.

[110] Wolfgang J. Mommsen, 'Bismarck, the Concert of Europe, and the Future of West Africa, 1883–1885', in [301] pp. 151–70: see [69].

[111] Daniel Pick, *Faces of Degeneration: a European Disorder, c.1848–c.1918* (Cambridge, 1989).

[112] Andrew Porter, 'Cambridge, Keswick and late Nineteenth-Century Attitudes to Africa', *JICH*, V (1976), 5–34: important study of the relationship between theology, culture, conversion and race in British evangelical thought.

[113] Andrew Porter, 'Evangelical Enthusiasm, Missionary Motivation and West Africa in the late Nineteenth Century: the Career of G.W. Brooke', *JICH*, VI (1977), 23–46: illuminates key changes in Protestant thinking about the links between the spread of Christianity and western expansion.

[114] A.N. Porter, 'Lord Salisbury, Foreign Policy and Domestic Finance, 1860–1900', in Robert Blake and Hugh Cecil (eds), *Salisbury: The Man and His Policies* (London, 1987), pp. 148–84.

[115] Andrew Porter, 'Religion and Empire: British Expansion in the long Nineteenth Century 1780–1914', *JICH*, XX (1992), 370–90: surveys the changing pattern of relations between missions and the state.

[116] Bernard Porter, *Britain, Europe and the World 1850–1982* (London, 1983): stimulating interpretative essay on Britain's relative 'decline', and the constraints which made imperial initiatives inescapable but damaging.

[117] Jeffrey Richards (ed.), *Imperialism and Juvenile Literature* (Manchester, 1989).

[118] G.N. Sanderson, *England, Europe and the Upper Nile, 1882–1899* (Edinburgh, 1965): the outstanding account of British diplomacy in a critical area of European confrontation.

[119] G.N. Sanderson, 'The Origins and Significance of the Anglo-French Confrontation at Fashoda, 1898', in [303] pp. 285–331.

[120] G.N. Sanderson, 'The European Partition of Africa: Origins and Dynamics', in [316] pp. 96–158 and 772–82: a very fine attempt to establish the phases and the relative importance of different forces.

[121] Wm H. Schneider, *An Empire for the Masses. The French Popular Image of Africa, 1870–1900* (Westport, Conn., 1982): with [76], provides a useful introduction to French racial attitudes.

[122] Wm H. Schneider, 'Geographical Reform and Municipal Imperialism in France, 1870–80', in [309] pp. 90–117.

[123] G.R. Searle, *The Quest for National Efficiency: a Study in British Politics and Political Thought, 1899–1914* (Oxford, 1971; repr. 1990): illuminates many of the metropolitan fears of the period and their relationship to imperial concerns, in ways relevant not only to Britain.

[124] Bernard Semmel, *The Governor Eyre Controversy* (London, 1962): the standard account of British reactions to the 'Morant Bay rebellion' by blacks in Jamaica, 1865.

86

[125] Brian Stanley, *The Bible and the Flag. Protestant Missions and British Imperialism in the Nineteenth and Twentieth Centuries* (Leicester, 1990): very informative survey, focusing on missionary intentions rather than impact.

[126] H. Pogge von Strandmann, 'Consequences of the Foundation of the German Empire: Colonial Expansion and the Process of Political-Economic Rationalization', in [301] pp. 105–20: see [69].

[127] Marvin Swartz, *The Politics of British Foreign Policy in the Era of Disraeli and Gladstone* (London, 1985): argues for the importance of integrating party-political calculation and domestic interest group pressures with analyses of diplomacy.

[128] A.J.P. Taylor, *Germany's First Bid for Colonies 1884–85: A Move in Bismarck's European Policy* (London, 1938): argues for colonial initiatives rooted in narrowly European, anti-British concerns.

[129] Patrick J.N. Tuck, *French Catholic Missionaries and the Politics of Imperialism in Vietnam, 1857–1914* (Liverpool UP, 1987): a most valuable collection of documents, with extended commentary.

[130] J.P. Tudesco, *Missionaries and French Imperialism: the Role of Catholic Missionaries in French Colonial Expansion, 1880–1905* (1985).

[131] H.A. Turner, 'Bismarck's Imperialist Venture: Anti-British in Origin?' in [302] pp. 47–82: gives the answer 'no'.

[132] P.R. Warhurst, *Anglo-Portuguese Relations in South Central Africa 1890–1900* (London, 1962): complements [25–26], [33], [67], [81] and [86].

[133] H.-U. Wehler, 'Bismarck's Imperialism, 1862–1890', *P&P*, 48 (1970), 119–55.

[134] H.-U. Wehler, 'Industrial growth and Early German imperialism', in [317] pp. 71–92.

[135] H.-U. Wehler, *The German Empire 1871–1918* (1973; English translation, Leamington Spa, 1985).

# 3 'Metropolitan' Explanations – Social and Economic

[136] C.M. Andrew, 'The French Colonialist Movement during the Third Republic: the Unofficial Mind of Imperialism', *TRHS*, XXVI (1976), with [137]-[140], demonstrates conclusively the very limited links between colonial enthusiasm and business interests before 1914.

[137] C.M. Andrew and A.S. Kanya-Forstner, 'The French "Colonial Party": its Composition, Aims and Influence, 1885–1914', *HJ*, 14 (1971), 99–128.

[138] C.M. Andrew and A.S. Kanya-Forstner, 'The Groupe Colonial in the French Chamber of Deputies, 1892–1932', *HJ*, 17 (1974), 837–66.

[139] C.M. Andrew, P. Grupp and A.S. Kanya-Forstner, 'Le mouvement colonial français et ses principales personnalités', *RFHOM*, LXII (1975), 640–73.

[140] C.M. Andrew and A.S. Kanya-Forstner, 'French Business and the French Colonialists', *HJ*, 19 (1976), 981–1000.

[141] R.T. Anstey, *Britain and the Congo in the Nineteenth Century* (Oxford, 1962).

[142] M. Bastide, 'La diplomatie française et la révolution chinoise de 1911', in [146] pp. 127–52.

[143] W.G. Beasley, *Japanese Imperialism 1894–1945* (Oxford, 1991).

[144] Ian D. Black, *A Gambling Style of Government: the Establishment of the Chartered Company's Rule in Sabah, 1878–1915* (Kuala Lumpur, 1983).

[145] Richard Bosworth, *Italy and the Approach of the First World War* (London, 1983).

[146] Jean Bouvier and René Girault (eds), *L'Impérialisme français d'avant 1914* (Paris, 1976): discusses the relationship between French investment overseas after 1870 and concepts of imperialism.

[147] M.E. Chamberlain, 'Imperialism and Social Reform', in [298] pp. 148–67: suggestive as to the importance of distinguishing between 'social imperialism' and other links between social programmes and imperial activity.

[148] Stanley Chapman, *The Rise of Merchant Banking* (London, 1984).

[149] Stanley Chapman, *Merchant Enterprise in Britain: From the Industrial Revolution to World War I* (Cambridge, 1992).

[150] Catherine Coquery-Vidrovitch, *Le Congo au temps des grandes compagnies concessionaires, 1898–1930* (Paris, 1972).

[151] P.L. Cottrell, *British Overseas Investment in the Nineteenth Century* (London, 1975): excellent short general account, including demonstration of the mismatch between capital exports and colonial acquisitions.

[152] R.P.T. Davenport-Hines and Geoffrey Jones (eds), *British Business in Asia since 1870* (Cambridge, 1989).

[153] Ronald Dreyer, *The Official Mind of Imperialism: British and Cape Government perceptions of German rule in Namibia . . . (1890–1896)*, (Essen, 1987).

[154] M. Edelstein, 'Foreign Investment and Empire 1860–1914', in R. Floud and D.M. McCloskey (eds), *The Economic History of Britain since 1700*, vol. 2 (Cambridge, 1981): useful discussion of the returns to Britain.

[155] E.W. Edwards, *British Diplomacy and Finance in China, 1895–1914* (Oxford, 1987).

[156] Geoff Eley, 'Defining Social Imperialism: Use and Abuse of an Idea', *Social History*, 3 (1976), 265–89: a valuable article by a historian of Germany highly critical of Wehler's usage of the term.

[157] S. Elwitt, *The Making of the Third Republic: Class and Politics in France 1868–1884* (Baton Rouge, 1975).

[158] S. Elwitt, *The Third Republic Defended: Bourgeois Reform in France 1880–1914* (Baton Rouge, 1986/7).

[159] J.H. Esterhuyse, *South West Africa 1880–1894: The Establishment of German Authority in South West Africa* (Cape Town, 1968).

[160] C. Feinstein, 'Britain's Overseas Investments in 1913', *EcHR*, 43 (1990), 288–95.

[161] D.K. Fieldhouse, *Unilever Overseas: The Anatomy of a Multinational 1895–1965* (London/Stanford, 1978).

[162] John E. Flint, *Sir George Goldie and the Making of Nigeria* (London, 1960).

[163] I.L.D. Forbes, 'German Informal Imperialism in South America before 1914', *EcHR*, 31 (1978), 384–98.

[164] I.L.D. Forbes, 'Social Imperialism and Wilhelmine Germany', *HJ*, 22 (1979), 331–49: shows the irrelevance of social imperial calculations to expansion in South America.

[165] John S. Galbraith, *Crown and Charter: The Early Years of the British South Africa Company* (Berkeley/London, 1974).

[166] John S. Galbraith, *Mackinnon and East Africa 1878–1895* (Cambridge, 1972).

[167] Jose Harris and Pat Thane, 'British and European Bankers 1880–1914: an "aristocratic bourgeoisie"?', in P. Thane, G. Crossick and R. Floud (eds), *The Power of the Past* (Cambridge, 1984), pp. 215–34: a useful introduction to current work on the status and influence of financiers.

[168] H.H. Herwig, *Germany's Vision of Empire in Venezuela, 1871–1914* (Princeton, 1986).

[169] A.G. Hopkins, 'Imperial Business in Africa', Pts 1 & 2, *JAH*, 17 (1976), 29–48, 267–90.

[170] William G. Hynes, *The Economics of Empire: Britain, Africa and the New Imperialism 1870–1895* (London, 1979): a perceptive study of mercantile expectations, commercial agitation and economic fluctuations.

[171] W.G. Hynes, 'British Mercantile Attitudes towards Imperial Expansion', *HJ*, 19 (1976), 969–79: see with [170] and [232].

[172] Charles A. Jones, *International Business in the Nineteenth Century: The Rise and Fall of a Cosmopolitan Bourgeoisie* (London, 1987).

[173] Stephanie Jones, *Two Centuries of Overseas Trading: The Origins and Growth of the Inchcape Group* (London, 1986).

[174] Paul Kennedy, 'German Colonial Expansion: has the "Manipulated Social Imperialism" been Ante-dated?', *P&P*, 54 (1972), 134–41: argues that 'social imperialism' is irrelevant to an understanding of Bismarck's actions, but may be important after *c*.1897.

[175] Paul M. Kennedy, *The Samoan Tangle: A Study in Anglo-German-American Relations, 1878–1900* (Dublin, 1974): a fine study of Pacific entanglements, and illustrates the argument in [174].

[176] G. Kurgan-Van Hentenryk, *Léopold II et les groupes financiers belges en Chine: la politique royale et ses prolongements, 1895–1914* (Brussels, 1972).

[177] John F. Laffey, 'Roots of French Imperialism in the Nineteenth Century: The Case of Lyon', *French Historical Studies*, VI (1969), 78–92.

[178] John F. Laffey, 'Municipal Imperialism in France: The Lyon Chamber of Commerce, 1900–1914', *Proceedings of the American Philosophical Society*, 119 (1975), 8–23.

[179] John F. Laffey, 'Lyonnais Imperialism in the Far East, 1900–1938', *MAS*, 10 (1976), 235–48.

[180] David S. Landes, *Bankers and Pashas* (London, 1958): illuminating study of growth of French financial influence in Egypt.

[181] David Landes, *The Unbound Prometheus. Technological Change and Industrial Development in Western Europe from 1750 to the Present* (Cambridge, 1969).

[182] H. Lebovics, *The Alliance of Iron and Wheat in the Third Republic, 1860–1914: Origins of the New Conservatism* (Baton Rouge, 1988).

[183] Robert Lee, *France and the Exploitation of China 1885–1901: A Study in Economic Imperialism* (Hong Kong, 1989).

[184] Martin Lynn, 'From Sail to Steam: The Impact of the Steamship Services on the British Palm Oil Trade with West Africa, 1850–1890', *JAH*, 30 (1989), 227–45: valuable on the commercial and technological underpinnings of imperial expansion.

[185] Martin Lynn, 'Bristol, West Africa and the Nineteenth-Century Palm Oil Trade', *Historical Research*, 64 (1991), 359–74.

[186] David McLean, *Britain and Her Buffer State: the Collapse of the Persian Empire, 1890–1914* (London, 1979).

[187] David McLean, 'Finance and "Informal Empire" before the First World War', *EcHR*, 29 (1976), 291–305.

[188] W.J. Mommsen, *Egypt and the Middle East in German Foreign Policy 1870–1914* (forthcoming).

[189] F.F. Muller, *Deutschland – Zanzibar – Ostafrika 1884–1890* (Berlin, 1959); important study of German commercial and chartered company activity.

[190] J. Forbes Munro, 'Shipping Subsidies and Railway Guarantees: William Mackinnon, Eastern Africa and the Indian Ocean, 1860–1893', *JAH*, 28 (1987), 209–30.

[191] J.B.S. Neil-Tomlinson, The Mozambique Chartered Company 1892 to 1910 (unpub. Ph.D. thesis, Univ. of London, 1987).

[192] Colin Newbury, 'On the Margins of Empire: The Trade of Western Africa, 1875–1890', in [301] pp. 35–58: argues that the seriousness of commercial depression and the inability of merchants to meet it without government assistance have been exaggerated.

[193] S.M. Persell, *The French Colonial Lobby, 1899–1938* (Stanford, c. 1983).

[194] R.V. Pierard, 'The German Colonial Society', in [306] pp. 19–38.

[195] D.C.M. Platt (ed.), *Business Imperialism 1840–1930: An Inquiry Based on British Experience in Latin America* (Oxford, 1977): an important collection of studies suggesting that Britain's presence involved neither 'informal imperialism' nor enforced dependency.

[196] D.C.M. Platt, 'Canada and Argentina: the First Preference of the British Investor, 1904–1914', *JICH*, XIII (1985), 77–92: illustrates the irrelevance of formal imperial control to changing directions of British investment.

[197] D.C.M. Platt, 'British Portfolio Investment Overseas before 1870: Some Doubts', *EcHR*, 33 (1980), 1–16.

[198] D.C.M. Platt, *Britain's Investment Overseas on the Eve of the First World War* (London, 1986).

[199] Sidney Pollard, *Peaceful Conquest: the Industrialization of Europe 1760–1970* (Oxford, 1981).

[200] Sidney Pollard, *Britain's Prime and Britain's Decline: the British Economy*

*1870–1914* (London, 1989): see especially ch.2, discussing the domestic implications for Britain of large investments abroad.

[201] Andrew Porter, *Victorian Business, Shipping and Imperial Policy: Donald Currie, the Castle Line and Southern Africa* (Woodbridge/New York, 1986).

[202] A.N. Porter, 'Britain, the Cape Colony and Natal, 1870–1914: Capital, Shipping and the Imperial Connection', *EcHR*, 34 (1980), 554–77.

[203] B.M. Ratcliffe, 'Commerce and Empire: Manchester Merchants and West Africa, 1873–1895', *JICH*, VII (1979), 293–320.

[204] Nini Rogers, 'The Abyssinian Expedition of 1867–1868: Disraeli's Imperialism or James Murray's War?', *HJ*, 27 (1984), 129–49: rejects [84] in favour of an explanation based on traditional official perceptions.

[205] Bernard Semmel, *Imperialism and Social Reform: English Social-Imperial Thought 1895–1914* (London, 1960): still essential reading, not just for the British case.

[206] Joseph Smith, 'American Expansionism during the Gilded Age, 1865–98', in [314] pp. 83–99: brief but useful introduction to the debate.

[207] Steven R.B. Smith, 'The Centenary of the London Chamber of Commerce: Its Origins and Early Policy', *London Journal*, 8 (1982), 156–70. See also his 'Public Opinion, the Navy and the City of London: the Drive for British Naval Expansion in the late Nineteenth Century', *War and Society*, 9 (1991), 29–50, for the London Chamber in action.

[208] W.D. Smith, 'The Ideology of German Colonialism, 1840–1906', *Journal of Modern History*, 46 (1974), 641–62: in the light of German thinking, questions the value of appeals to social imperialist explanation.

[209] J. Stengers, 'Léopold II entre l'Extrême-Orient et l'Afrique, 1875–1876', in *La Conférence de Géographie de 1876: Recueil d'études* (Brussels, 1976), pp. 303–73.

[210] H.P. von Strandmann, 'Domestic Origins of Germany's Colonial Expansion under Bismarck', *P&P*, 42 (1969), 140–59.

[211] S. Sugiyama, *Japan's Industrialization in the World Economy 1859–1899* (London, 1988): explains Japan's successful resistance and adaptation to European expansion.

[212] J. Thobie, 'Finance et politique: le refus en France de l'emprunt ottoman de 1910', in [146] pp. 188–214.

[213] C. Trebilcock, *The Industrialization of the Continental Powers 1780–1914* (London, 1981).

[214] K.G. Treggoning, *Under Chartered Company Rule: North Borneo, 1881–1946* (London, 1958).

[215] Leroy Vail, 'Mozambique's Chartered Companies: the Rule of the Feeble', *JAH*, 17 (1976), 389–416.

[216] H. Washausen, *Hamburg und die Kolonialpolitik des deutschen Reiches 1880 bis 1890* (Hamburg, 1968).

[217] R.A. Webster, *Industrial Imperialism in Italy 1908–1915* (Berkeley/

London, 1975): particularly important for its examination of links between the ambitions of financial groups and heavy industry, and foreign policy towards the eastern Mediterranean/Ottoman empire.

[218] Charles Wilson, *The History of Unilever*, 2 vols (London, 1954).

## 4 'Peripheral' Explanations

[219] J.F.A. Ajayi, *Christian Missions in Nigeria 1841–1891* (London, 1965).

[220] Robert Aldrich, *The French Presence in the South Pacific, 1842–1940* (London, 1990).

[221] A.E. Atmore, 'The Extra-European Foundations of British Imperialism: Towards a Reassessment', in [298] pp. 106–25: outlines difficulties involved in the concept of 'collaboration' defined in [241].

[222] C.A. Bayly, *Imperial Meridian: The British Empire and the World, 1780–1830* (London, 1989).

[223] John Benyon, 'Overlords of Empire? British "Proconsular Imperialism" in comparative perspective', *JICH*, XIX (1991), 164–202.

[224] P.J. Cain, 'European Expansion Overseas 1830–1914', *History*, 59 (1974), 243–9: a useful critical review of [3].

[225] Donald Denoon, *Settler Capitalism* (Oxford, 1983): stimulating examination of the growth of extra-European centres of capitalist development, with their own potential for 'imperialist' expansion.

[226] John S. Galbraith, 'The "Turbulent Frontier" as a Factor in British Expansion', *Comparative Studies in Society and History*, II (1959–60), 150–68.

[227] John D. Hargreaves, *West Africa Partitioned:* I *The Loaded Pause 1885–89*, II *The Elephants and the Grass* (London, 1974, 1985): with [83], the most authoritative comprehensive account of European involvement in West African affairs.

[228] A.G. Hopkins, *An Economic History of West Africa* (London, 1973): a most important study, relevant here for linking the interplay of local and metropolitan economies to political change.

[229] A.G. Hopkins, 'The Victorians and Africa: a Reconsideration of the Occupation of Egypt, 1882', *JAH*, 27 (1986), 363–91: in reaction against [239], attempts to restore a central metropolitan economic interest into explanations of the making and resolution of the Egyptian crisis of 1875–82.

[230] W. Ross Johnston, *Sovereignty and Protection: A Study of British Jurisdictional Imperialism in the late Nineteenth Century* (Durham, NC, 1973): a most interesting and unjustly neglected study of the gradual extension of legal authority overseas.

[231] John Lonsdale, 'The European Scramble and Conquest in African History', in [316] pp. 680–766.

[232] Martin Lynn, 'The "imperialism of free trade" and the case of West Africa, *c.* 1830–*c.* 1870', *JICH*, XV (1986), 22–39: explains the conditions which make the concept inapplicable before 1870, cf. [171] and [237].

92

[233] Doug Munro and Stewart Firth, 'From Company Rule to Consular Control: Gilbert Island Labourers on German Plantations in Samoa, 1867–96', *JICH*, XVI (1987), 24–44.

[234] Colin Newbury, 'The Semantics of International Influence: Informal Empires Reconsidered', in Michael Twaddle (ed.), *Imperialism, The State and the Third World* (London, 1992): argues for analysing the growth of informal empire and controls in terms of transfers of technology in all its forms, rather than those of politics.

[235] A.D. Nzemeke, 'Free Trade and Territorial Partition in Nineteenth-century West Africa: Course and Outcome', in [301] pp. 59–68.

[236] A.D. Nzemeke, *British Imperialism and African Response: the Niger Valley, 1851–1905* (Paderborn, 1982).

[237] Jürgen Osterhammel, 'Semi-Colonialism and Informal Empire in Twentieth-Century China: towards a Framework for Analysis', in [313] pp. 290–314: with [232], offers stimulating suggestions as what particular relationships between weaker and stronger states may be defined as imperialistic.

[238] Gwyn Prins, *The Hidden Hippopotamus. Reappraisal in African History: The Early Colonial Experience in Western Zambia* (Cambridge, 1980).

[239] Ronald Robinson and John Gallagher, *Africa and the Victorians: the Official Mind of Imperialism* (London, 1961; 2nd edn, 1981).

[240] Ronald Robinson and John Gallagher, 'The Partition of Africa', in F.H. Hinsley (ed.), *The New Cambridge Modern History* vol. XI: *Material Progress and World-Wide Problems, 1870–1898* (Cambridge, 1962), pp. 593–640.

[241] Ronald Robinson, 'Non-European Foundations of European Imperialism: Sketch for a Theory of Collaboration', in [317] pp. 117–40.

[242] Ronald Robinson, 'European Imperialism and Indigenous Reactions in British West Africa, 1880–1914', in H.L. Wesseling (ed.), *Expansion and Reaction* (Leiden, 1978), pp. 141–63.

[243] Ronald Robinson, 'The Excentric Idea of Imperialism, with or without Empire', in [313] pp. 267–89.

[244] D.M. Schreuder, *The Scramble for Southern Africa, 1877–1895: the Politics of Partition Reappraised* (Cambridge, 1980).

[245] B. Schnapper, *La Politique et le commerce français dans le Golfe de Guinée de 1838 à 1871* (Paris, 1961).

[246] J. Stengers, 'Leopold II and the Association Internationale du Congo', in [301] pp. 229–44.

[247] Roger C. Thompson, *Australian Imperialism in the Pacific: The Expansionist Era, 1820–1920* (Melbourne, 1980).

[248] D. Washbrook, 'Law, State and Agrarian Society in Colonial India', *MAS*, 15 (1981), 649–721.

## 5 Other Recent Approaches

[249] David Anderson and Richard Grove (eds), *Conservation in Africa: People, Policies and Practice* (Cambridge, 1987).

[250] David Anderson and David Killingray (eds), *Policing the Empire: Government, Authority and Control, 1830–1940* (Manchester, 1991).

[251] Talal Asad (ed.), *Anthropology and the Colonial Encounter* (London, 1973).

[252] K. Ballhatchet, *Race, Sex and Class under the Raj: Imperial Attitudes and Polices and their Critics, 1793–1905* (London, 1980).

[253] C.A. Bayly, *Indian Society and the Making of the British Empire* (Cambridge, 1988).

[254] M.T. Berger, 'Imperialism and Sexual Exploitation: a Review Article'; and R. Hyam, 'A Reply', *JICH*, XVII (1988), 83–9, 90–8.

[255] J.G. Butcher, *The British in Malaya, 1880–1941: the Social History of a European Community in Colonial South-East Asia* (Kuala Lumpur, 1979).

[256] P.J. Cain and A.G. Hopkins, 'The Political Economy of British Expansion Overseas, 1750–1914', *EcHR*, 33 (1980), 463–90.

[257] P.J. Cain and A.G. Hopkins, 'Gentlemanly Capitalism and British Expansion Overseas. I The Old Colonial System, 1688–1850', and 'II New Imperialism, 1850–1945', *EcHR*, 39 (1986), 501–25, and 40 (1987), 1–26.

[258] Peter Cain, 'J.A. Hobson, Financial Capitalism and Imperialism in Late Victorian and Edwardian England', in A.N. Porter and R.F. Holland (eds), *Money, Finance and Empire 1790–1860* (London, 1985), 1–27.

[259] P.J. Cain and A.G. Hopkins, *British Imperialism I Innovation and Expansion, 1688–1914; II Crisis and Deconstruction 1914–1990*, (London, 1993).

[260] H. Callaway, *Gender, Culture and Empire: European Women in Colonial Nigeria* (London, 1987).

[261] Nupur Chaudhuri and Margaret Strobel (eds), *Western Women and Imperialism: Complicity and Resistance* (Bloomington, 1992).

[262] W.G. Clarence-Smith, ' "The Imperialism of Beggars": the Role of the Less Developed Powers in the Nineteenth Century Scramble for Colonies', in *The City and the Empire* vol. 2. (Institute of Commonwealth Studies: London, 1987).

[263] W.B. Cohen, *Rulers of Empire. The French Colonial Service in Africa* (Stanford, 1971)

[264] Jean Copans (ed.), *Anthropologie et impérialisme* (Paris, 1975).

[265] M.J. Daunton, ' "Gentlemanly Capitalism" and British Industry 1820–1914', *P&P*, 122 (1989), 119–58: argues that financial and industrial interests cannot be separated in the way proposed by [257].

[266] Lance E. Davis and Robert A. Huttenback, *Mammon and the Pursuit of Empire: The Political Economy of British Imperialism, 1860–1912* (Cambridge, 1986).

[267] L.H. Gann and Peter Duignan, *The Rulers of British Africa 1870–1914* (Stanford, 1978).

[268] L.H. Gann and Peter Duignan, *The Rulers of German Africa 1884–1914* (Stanford, 1977).

[269] L.H. Gann and Peter Duignan, *The Rulers of Belgian Africa 1884–1914* (Princeton, 1979).

[270] Richard H. Grove, 'Colonial Conservation, Ecological Hegemony and Popular Resistance: Towards a Global Synthesis', in [309] pp. 15–50.

[271] Robert Heussler, *British Rule in Malaya: the Malayan Civil Service and its Predecessors 1867–1942* (Oxford, 1981).

[272] A.G. Hopkins, 'Review Article. Accounting for the British Empire', *JICH*, XVI (1988), 234–47: a well-directed critical review of [266].

[273] Ronald Inden, 'Orientalist Constructions of India', *MAS*, 20 (1986), 401–46.

[274] Ronald Inden, *Imagining India* (Oxford, 1990).

[275] Paul Kennedy, *The Rise and Fall of British Naval Mastery* (London, 1976; 3rd edn, 1991).

[276] Paul Kennedy, 'Debate. The Costs and Benefits of British Imperialism 1846–1914', *P&P*, 125 (1989), 186–92: takes issue with the interpretation of imperial defence costs in [280]; response in Patrick K. O'Brien, 'Reply', ibid., 192–9.

[277] A.J.H. Latham, *The International Economy and the Underdeveloped World, 1865–1914* (London, 1978): portrays 'the capitalism of the developed world expanding outwards', bringing new and mutually advantageous opportunities 'to the indigenous capitalism of the undeveloped world'. Cf. [279] and [295].

[278] Timothy Mitchell, *Colonising Egypt* (Cambridge, 1988).

[279] J. Forbes Munro, *Africa and the International Economy 1800–1960* (London, 1976): focuses on 'the erosion of African economic autonomy' in the interests of the western industrialised world.

[280] Patrick K. O'Brien, 'The Costs and Benefits of British Imperialism 1846–1914', *P&P*, 120 (1988), 163–200: endorses [266], and those contemporaries who argued either that imperialism was a serious drain on British resources or that it warped British social development.

[281] Frank Perlin, 'Proto-industrialization and Pre-colonial South Asia', *P&P*, 98 (1983), 30–95: critical of Wallerstein for ignoring the realities of extra-European economies, especially the local merchant capitalisms and domestic manufacturing of the seventeenth and eighteenth centuries. These were only subsequently disrupted by Europe's increasing hegemony, and then often in ways exactly comparable to changes taking place inside Europe itself.

[282] Andrew Porter, 'Review Article. A Regiment of Rulers', *JICH*, IX (1981), 331–40: offers suggestions as to where the work of [267–69] might be built upon.

[283] Andrew Porter, 'The Balance Sheet of Empire, 1850–1914', *HJ*, 31 (1988), 685–99: argues that [266] has failed to understand the empire it is assessing, and therefore many of its conclusions need serious reconsideration.

[284] Andrew Porter, '"Gentlemanly Capitalism" and Empire: the British Experience since 1750?', *JICH*, XVIII (1990), 265–95: argues that the diversity of imperial interests and dynamics cannot be satisfactorily accommodated by the concept as presented in [257].

[285] Andrew Porter, 'The South African War (1899–1902): Context and Motive Reconsidered', *JAH*, 31 (1990), 43–57: with reference to recent literature, outlines difficulties for predominantly economic accounts of the war.

[286] David Prochaska, *Making Algeria French: Colonialism in Bone, 1870–1920* (Cambridge, 1990).

[287] L. Pyenson, *Cultural Imperialism and Exact Sciences: German Expansion Overseas, 1900–1930* (New York, 1985): from the evidence of German scientific activity in W. Samoa, Argentina and China, argues for the emergence by 1914 of an official strategy of cultural penetration aimed at imperial prestige and ultimate political control.

[288] T.O. Ranger, 'From Humanism to the Science of Man: Colonialism in Africa and the Understanding of Alien Societies', *TRHS*, 26 (1976), 115–41.

[289] Edward W. Said, *Orientalism* (London, 1978/1985): the polemical, politically-engaged work of a literary scholar, and now something of a cult book, it is nevertheless a compelling study. Most recently, see his *Culture and Imperialism* (London, 1993).

[290] Woodruff D. Smith, 'Anthropology and German Colonialism', in [306] pp. 39–58.

[291] Robert A. Stafford, *Scientist of Empire: Sir Roderick Murchison, Scientific Exploration and Victorian Imperialism* (Cambridge, 1989).

[292] George W. Stocking (ed.), *Functionalism Historicized. Essays on British Social Anthropology* [*History of Anthropology*, vol. 2], (Wisconsin, 1984): along with subsequent volumes, contains essays dissecting the links of anthropology with imperialism.

[293] Margaret Strobel, *European Women and the Second British Empire* (Bloomington, 1991).

[294] I. Wallerstein, *The Modern World System*: I *Capitalist Agriculture and the Origins of the European World-economy in the Sixteenth Century* (New York, 1974); II *Mercantilism and the Consolidation of the European World-economy, 1600–1750* (New York, 1980); III *The Second Era of Great Expansion of the Capitalist World Economy, 1730–1840s* (San Diego/London, 1989).

[295] I. Wallerstein, *The Capitalist World Economy. Essays* (Cambridge, 1979): collected studies illustrative of the world economy's evolution to the present.

## 6 Miscellaneous

[296] Jerome Ch'en, *China and the West: Society and Culture 1815–1937* (London, 1979).

[297] Clarence B. Davis and Kenneth E. Wilburn (eds), *Railway Imperialism* (Westport, Conn., 1991): studies of European railway building and 'informal' imperialism.

[298] C.C. Eldridge (ed.), *British Imperialism in the Nineteenth Century* (London, 1984): valuable collection of essays, especially with reference to questions of continuity, discontinuity and coherence.

[299] P.C. Emmer and H.L. Wesseling (eds), *Reappraisals in Overseas History: Essays on Post-War Historiography about European Expansion* (Leiden, 1979): extensive commentaries on recent historical writing.

[300] James Foreman-Peck, *A History of the World Economy: International Economic Relations Since 1850* (Brighton, 1983).

[301] Stig Förster, Wolfgang J. Mommsen and Ronald Robinson (eds), *Bismarck, Europe and Africa: The Berlin Africa Conference 1884–1885 and the Onset of Partition* (Oxford, 1988): very important collection of essays touching (title notwithstanding) all aspects of Europe's involvement with Africa, 1860–1918, and an invaluable guide to recent German publications.

[302] Prosser Gifford and Wm Roger Louis (eds), *Britain and Germany in Africa: Imperial Rivalry and Colonial Rule* (New Haven, 1967): like [303], includes substantial chapters by different authors on Europe's involvement in Africa's partition and colonisation.

[303] Prosser Gifford and Wm Roger Louis (eds), *France and Britain in Africa: Imperial Rivalry and Colonial Rule* (New Haven, 1971).

[304] David Gillard, *The Struggle for Asia 1828–1914: A Study in British and Russian Imperialism* (London, 1977).

[305] V.J. Kiernan, *The Lords of Human Kind: European Attitudes to the Outside World in the Imperial Age* (rev. edn, Harmondsworth, 1972).

[306] Arthur J. Knoll and Lewis H. Gann (eds), *Germans in the Tropics: Essays in German Colonial History* (Westport, Conn., 1987): collection of miscellaneous but useful studies, including [194] and [290].

[307] Robin Law, 'Imperialism and Partition', *JAH*, 24 (1983), 101–4.

[308] David N. Livingstone, *The Geographical Tradition: Episodes in the History of a Contested Enterprise* (Oxford, 1992): for a guide to debate and recent literature about the social context of science and knowledge as power, see ch.7: 'A "Sternly Practical" Pursuit. Geography, Race and Empire'.

[309] John M. MacKenzie (ed.), *Imperialism and the Natural World* (Manchester, 1990).

[310] B.R. Mitchell, *Abstract of British Historical Statistics* (Cambridge, 1962: 2nd edn, 1988).

[311] B.R. Mitchell, *European Historical Statistics 1750–1975* (2nd rev. edn, London, 1981).

[312] B.R. Mitchell, *International Historical Statistics: Africa and Asia* (London, 1982); *The Americas and Australasia* (London, 1983).

[313] Wolfgang J. Mommsen and Jurgen Osterhammel (eds), *Imperialism and After: Continuities and Discontinuities* (London, 1986): although focusing chiefly on the twentieth century, contains much of relevance, especially in its discussions of theories, the concept of 'informal empire', and the relation of 'imperialism' to the changing international balance of power.

[314] Peter Morris (ed.), *Africa, America and Central Asia: Formal and Informal Empire in the Nineteenth Century* (Exeter, 1984): includes useful essays on southern Africa and Russia in Central Asia as well as [206].

[315] John A. Moses and Paul M. Kennedy (eds), *Germany in the Pacific and*

*Far East, 1870–1914* (St Lucia, 1977): an excellent, wide-ranging collection of essays.

[316] Roland Oliver and G.N. Sanderson (eds), *The Cambridge History of Africa* Vol. 6 *c.1870–c.1905* (Cambridge, 1985): highly authoritative and very comprehensive guide to Africa's history during the European Scramble and Partition.

[317] Roger Owen and Bob Sutcliffe (eds), *Studies in the Theory of Imperialism* (London, 1972): a very important series of essays and records of discussions, in which eminent historians considered the nature, purpose and utility of different theories.

[318] Paul B. Rich, *Race and Empire in British Politics* (2nd edn, Cambridge, 1990): chs 1–2 are useful for the years before 1914.

[319] Jonathan D. Spence, *The Search for Modern China* (London, 1990).

[320] D.J.M. Tate, *The Making of Modern South-East Asia*: Vol. I *The European Conquest* (Oxford U.P., 1971; rev. edn, 1977): exceptionally full narrative, with maps and chronologies.

[321] H.L. Wesseling and J.A. de Moor (eds), *Imperialism and War: Essays on Colonial Wars in Asia and Africa*. [Comparative Studies in Overseas History Volume 8] (Leiden, 1989): a valuable collection of studies, paying particular attention to British, Dutch, French and Italian examples.

# List of Maps and Tables

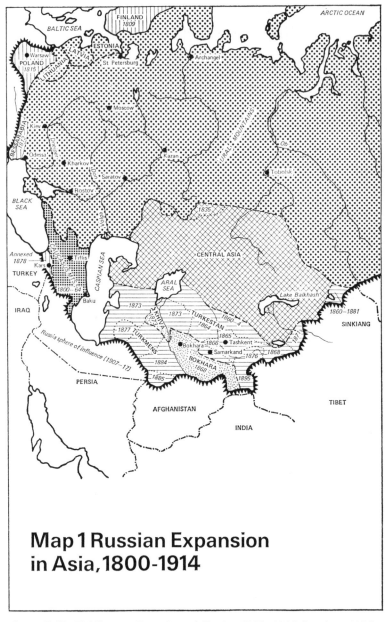

# Map 1 Russian Expansion
# in Asia, 1800-1914

*Source*: D.K. Fieldhouse, *Economics and Empire, 1830–1914* (London, 1984), pp.480–1.

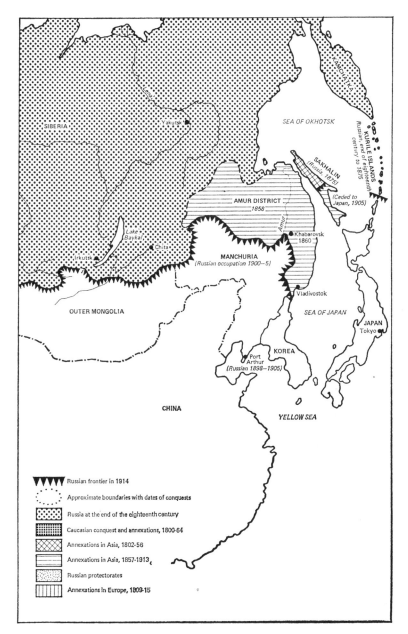

SIBERIA

Yakutsk

SEA OF OKHOTSK

KAMCHATKA

KURILE ISLANDS
Russian, end of eighteenth
century to 1875

SAKHALIN
(Russia, 1875)

AMUR DISTRICT
1858

(Ceded to
Japan, 1905)

Lake
Baykal

Chita

Khabarovsk
1860

Amur

Irkutsk

MANCHURIA
(Russian occupation 1900–5)

Vladivostok

OUTER MONGOLIA

SEA OF JAPAN

JAPAN
Tokyo

Port
Arthur
(Russian 1898–1905)

KOREA

CHINA

YELLOW SEA

Russian frontier in 1914

Approximate boundaries with dates of conquests

Russia at the end of the eighteenth century

Caucasian conquest and annexations, 1800-64

Annexations in Asia, 1802-56

Annexations in Asia, 1857-1913

Russian protectorates

Annexations in Europe, 1809-15

Maps 1–8 are reproduced by permission of Weidenfeld & Nicolson Ltd.

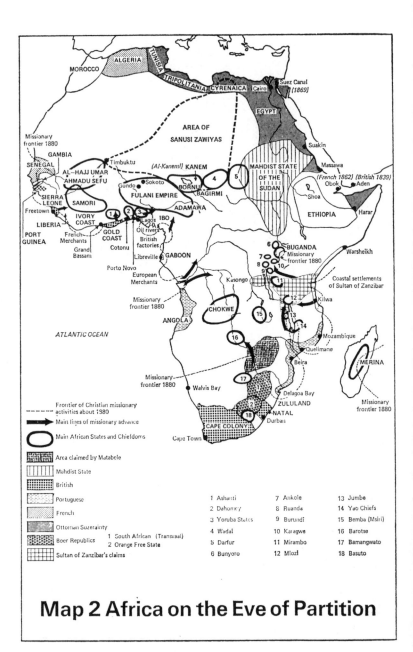

**Map 2 Africa on the Eve of Partition**

MOROCCO
ALGERIA
TUNISIA
TRIPOLITANIA
CYRENAICA
Cairo
Suez Canal (1869)
EGYPT
AREA OF SANUSI ZAWIYAS
Suakin
Massawa
(French 1862) (British 1839)
Obok Aden
Missionary frontier 1880
GAMBIA
SENEGAL
Timbuktu
(Al-Kanem!) KANEM
MAHDIST STATE OF THE SUDAN
AL-HAJJ UMAR
AHMADU SEFU
Gondo Sokoto
BORNU
BAGIRMI
4
5
Shoa
ETHIOPIA
Harar
SIERRA LEONE
Freetown
SAMORI
FULANI EMPIRE
ADAMAWA
LIBERIA
IVORY COAST
1
2
3
Lagos
IBO
Oil rivers
GOLD COAST
PORT GUINEA
French Merchants
Grand Bassam
Cotonu
British factories
BUGANDA
Missionary frontier 1880
Warsheikh
6
Porto Novo
Libreville GABOON
7
8
9
10
Coastal settlements of Sultan of Zanzibar
European Merchants
Kasongo
11
Missionary frontier 1880
12
Kilwa
CHOKWE
15
13
ANGOLA
14
ATLANTIC OCEAN
Mozambique
Quelimane
16
MERINA
Beira
Missionary frontier 1880
Walvis Bay
17
Missionary frontier 1880
Delagoa Bay
ZULULAND
NATAL
Durban
2
18
CAPE COLONY
Cape Town

Frontier of Christian missionary activities about 1880

Main lines of missionary advance

Main African States and Chiefdoms

Area claimed by Matabele

Mahdist State

British

Portuguese

French

Ottoman Suzerainty

Boer Republics   1 South African (Transvaal)
                 2 Orange Free State

Sultan of Zanzibar's claims

| | | |
|---|---|---|
| 1 Ashanti | 7 Ankole | 13 Jumbe |
| 2 Dahomey | 8 Ruanda | 14 Yao Chiefs |
| 3 Yoruba States | 9 Burundi | 15 Bemba (Msiri) |
| 4 Wadai | 10 Karagwe | 16 Barotse |
| 5 Darfur | 11 Mirambo | 17 Bamangwato |
| 6 Bunyoro | 12 Mlozi | 18 Basuto |

*Source*: Fieldhouse, *Economics and Empire, 1830–1914*, p. 482.

102

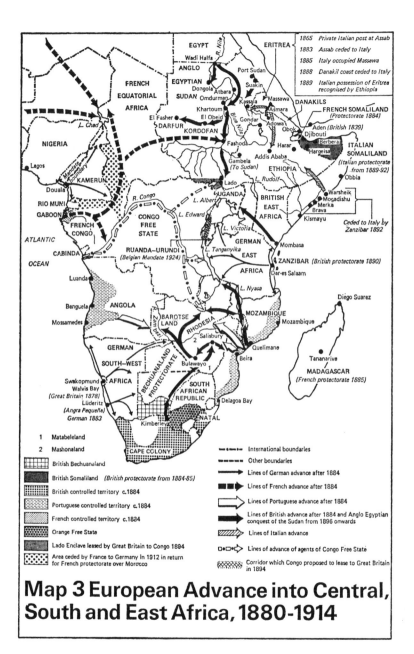

| | | |
|---|---|---|
| 1865 | Private Italian post at Assab |
| 1883 | Assab ceded to Italy |
| 1885 | Italy occupied Massawa |
| 1888 | Danakil coast ceded to Italy |
| 1889 | Italian possession of Eritrea recognised by Ethiopia |

1 Matabeleland
2 Mashonaland

British Bechuanaland
British Somaliland *(British protectorate from 1884-85)*
British controlled territory c.1884
Portuguese controlled territory c.1884
French controlled territory c.1884
Orange Free State
Lado Enclave leased by Great Britain to Congo 1894
Area ceded by France to Germany in 1912 in return for French protectorate over Morocco

International boundaries
Other boundaries
Lines of German advance after 1884
Lines of French advance after 1884
Lines of Portuguese advance after 1884
Lines of British advance after 1884 and Anglo Egyptian conquest of the Sudan from 1896 onwards
Lines of Italian advance
Lines of advance of agents of Congo Free State
Corridor which Congo proposed to lease to Great Britain in 1894

# Map 3 European Advance into Central, South and East Africa, 1880-1914

*Source*: Fieldhouse, *Economics and Empire, 1830–1914*, p. 483.

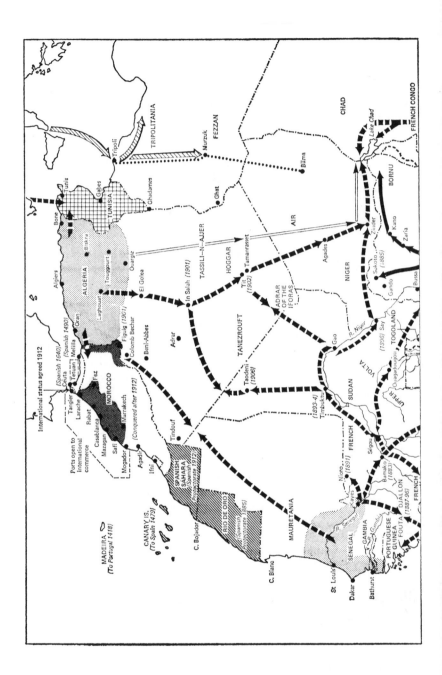

TRIPOLITANIA

FEZZAN

CHAD

FRENCH CONGO

Murzuk

Tripoli

Ghadames

Ghat

Bilma

Lake Chad

BORNU

Tunis

Gabes

Kano

Zaria

Bone

TUNISIA

TASSILI-N-AJER

AIR

Zinder

Sokoto

Gondo

Bussa

(1885)

Algiers

Biskra

ALGERIA

Touggourt

Ouargla

HOGGAR

Tamanrasset

Agades

NIGER

Oran

Laghouat

El Golea

In Salah (1901)

Tit

(1902)

ADRAR

OF THE

IFORAS

Gao

R. Niger

Say

(1896)

TOGOLAND

(Spanish 1640)

Ceuta

Figuig (1901)

Colomb Bechar

TANEZROUFT

VOLTA

Ouagadougou

UPPER

(Spanish 1490)

Tetuan

Melilla

Beni-Abbes

Adrar

Taodeni

(1906)

SUDAN

FRENCH

International status agreed 1912

Tangier

Fez

MOROCCO

Larache

Rabat

Marrakech

(Conquered after 1912)

Timbuktu

(1893-4)

Segou

Ports open to
international
commerce

Casablanca

Mazagan

Safi

Tindouf

FRENCH

Mogador

Agadir

Ifni

SPANISH

SAHARA

(Spanish Protectorate 1912)

Nioro

(1891)

Bamako

(1883)

FOUTA

DJALLON

(1887-96)

MADEIRA

(To Portugal 1418)

CANARY IS.

(To Spain 1479)

C. Bojador

RIO DE ORO

(Spanish
possession 1885)

MAURETANIA

Kayes

Senegal

SENEGAL

Gambia

GAMBIA

PORTUGUESE

GUINEA

C. Blanc

St Louis

Dakar

Bathurst

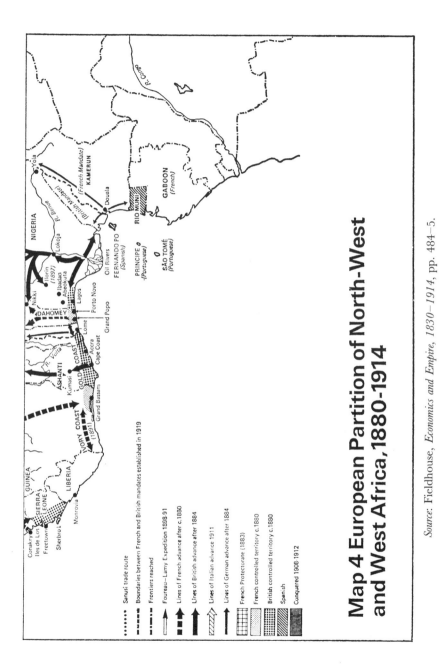

Source: Fieldhouse, *Economics and Empire, 1830–1914*, pp. 484–5.

## Map 4 European Partition of North-West and West Africa,1880-1914

Legend:

- Senusi trade route
- Boundaries between French and British mandates established in 1919
- Frontiers reached
- Foureau–Lamy Expedition 1898-91
- Lines of French advance after c.1880
- Lines of British advance after 1884
- Lines of Italian advance after 1884
- Lines of German advance after 1884
- French Protectorate (1883)
- French controlled territory c.1880
- British controlled territory c.1880
- Spanish
- Conquered 1908-1912

Map labels:

Conakry, Iles de Los, Freetown, Sherbro I., SIERRA LEONE, GUINEA, Monrovia, LIBERIA, IVORY COAST (1891), ASHANTI, Kumasi, Grand Bassam, GOLD COAST, R. Volta, Cape Coast, Accra, Grand Popo, Lome, DAHOMEY, Porto Novo, Lagos, Abeokuta, Ibadan, Ilorin (1897), Nikki, NIGERIA, Lokoja, R. Benue, Yola, Oil Rivers, FERNANDO PO (Spanish), PRINCIPE (Portuguese), SÃO TOMÉ (Portuguese), (French Mandate) (British Mandate), KAMERUN, Douala, RIO MUNI, GABOON (French), R. Congo

105

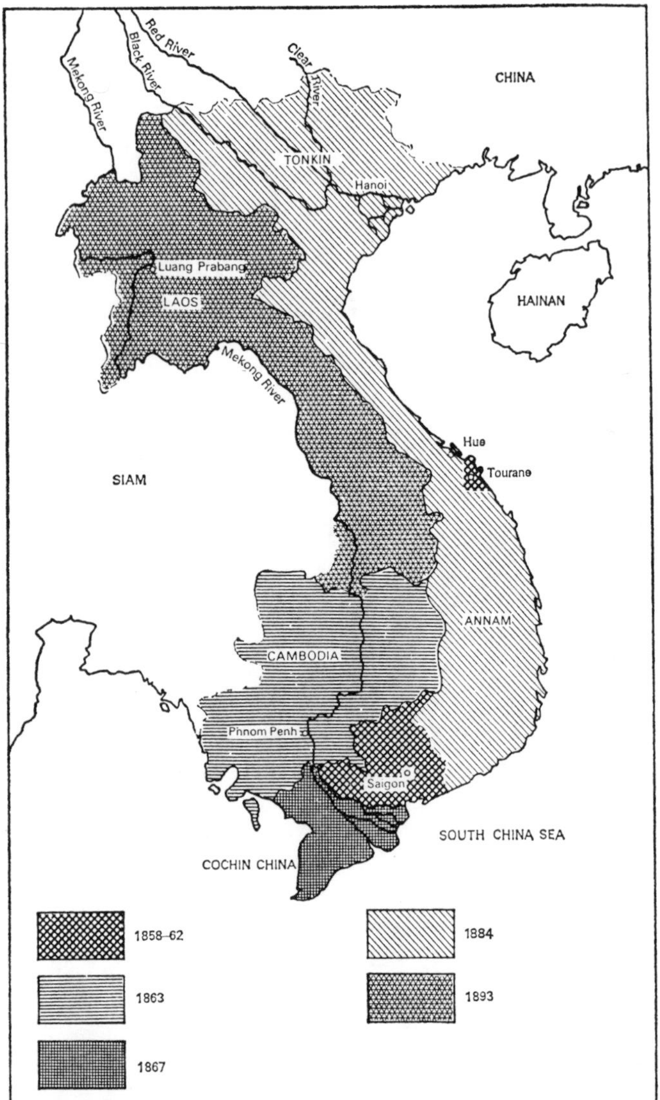
Red River
Black River
Mekong River
Clear River
CHINA
TONKIN
Hanoi
Luang Prabang
LAOS
HAINAN
Mekong River
Hue
Tourane
SIAM
ANNAM
CAMBODIA
Phnom Penh
Saigon
SOUTH CHINA SEA
COCHIN CHINA
1858–62
1884
1863
1893
1867

**Map 5 The Phases of French Conquest of Indo-China, 1858-93**

*Source*: Fieldhouse, *Economics and Empire, 1830–1914*, p. 486.

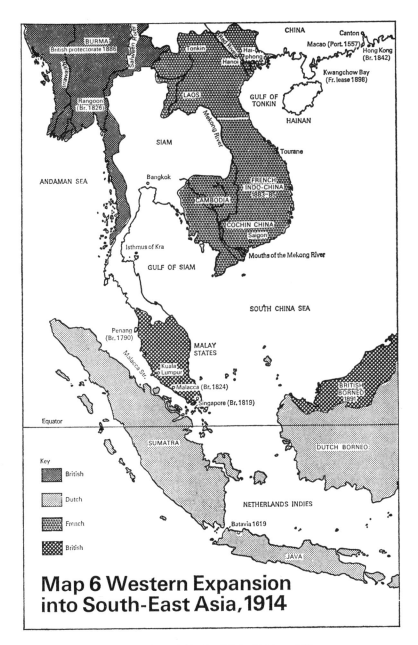

# Map 6 Western Expansion into South-East Asia, 1914

*Source*: Fieldhouse, *Economics and Empire, 1830–1914*, p. 487.

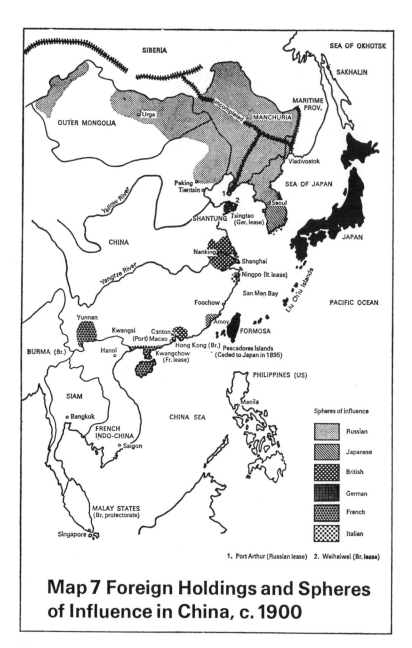

**Map 7 Foreign Holdings and Spheres of Influence in China, c. 1900**

*Source*: Fieldhouse, *Economics and Empire, 1830–1914*, p. 488.

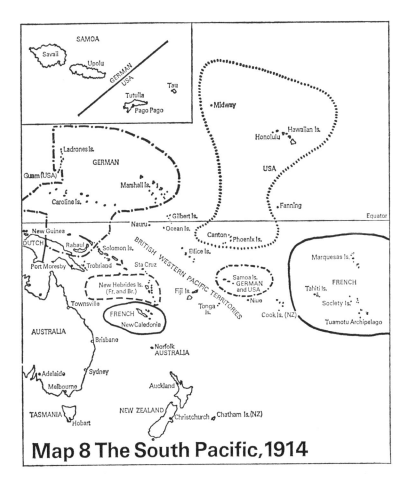

**Map 8 The South Pacific, 1914**

Labels within the map:

SAMOA
Savaii
Upolu
GERMAN
USA
Tutulla
Tau
Pago Pago
Midway
Hawaiian Is.
Honolulu
Ladrones Is.
GERMAN
Guam (USA)
USA
Marshall Is.
Caroline Is.
Fanning
Gilbert Is.
Nauru
Ocean Is.
Equator
New Guinea
Canton
Phoenix Is.
DUTCH
Rabaul
Solomon Is.
Ellice Is.
BRITISH WESTERN PACIFIC TERRITORIES
Port Moresby
Trobriand
Sta Cruz
Marquesas Is.
New Hebrides Is.
(Fr. and Br.)
Samoa Is.
GERMAN
and USA
FRENCH
Tahiti Is.
Fiji Is.
Niue
Society Is.
Townsville
Tonga Is.
FRENCH
New Caledonia
Cook Is. (NZ)
Tuamotu Archipelago
AUSTRALIA
Brisbane
Norfolk
AUSTRALIA
Adelaide
Sydney
Melbourne
Auckland
TASMANIA
Hobart
NEW ZEALAND
Christchurch
Chatham Is. (NZ)

*Source*: Fieldhouse, *Economics and Empire, 1830–1914*, p. 489.

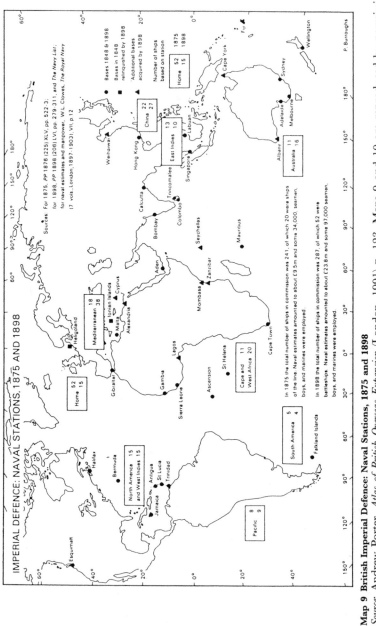

**Map 9  British Imperial Defence: Naval Stations, 1875 and 1898**
*Source*: Andrew Porter, *Atlas of British Overseas Expansion* (London, 1991) p. 123. Maps 9 and 10 are reproduced by permission of Routledge Ltd.

# International Telegraphs 1865–1914 (see Map 10)

| | | |
|---|---|---|
| 1 Port Arthur | 53 Suakin | 105 Cherbourg |
| 2 Taku | 54 Perim | 106 Rotterdam |
| 3 Chefoo | 55 Obok | 107 Goteborg |
| 4 Tsingtao | 56 Aden | 108 Nystad |
| 5 Shanghai | 57 Mombasa | 109 Farsund |
| 6 Nagasaki | 58 Zanzibar | 110 Peterhead |
| 7 Koyi | 59 Seychelles | 111 Azores |
| 8 Amami | 60 Mozambique | 112 Hearts Content/Placentia |
| 8 Nafa (Okinawa) | 61 Mojanga | 113 Halifax |
| 10 Pachung San (Miyako) | 62 Delagoa Bay | 114 Portsmouth |
| 11 Kelung | 63 Durban | 115 Boston |
| 12 Hong Kong | 64 Simon's Bay | 116 New York |
| 13 Manila | 65 Cape Town | 117 Bermuda |
| 14 Haiphong | 66 Swakopmund | 118 Nassau |
| 15 Hue | 67 Mossamedes | 119 Havana |
| 16 Saigon | 68 Benguela | 120 Port Royal |
| 17 Penang | 69 St Paul de Loanda | 121 San Juan |
| 18 Labuan | 70 Gabon | 122 St Thomas |
| 19 Sandakan | 71 Duala (Cameroon) | 123 Barbados |
| 20 Sarawak | 72 Bonny/Brass | 124 Trinidad |
| 21 Singapore | 73 Lagos | 125 Para |
| 22 Batavia | 74 Cotonou | 126 Maranhao |
| 23 Banjuwangi | 75 Accra | 127 Ceara |
| 24 Port Darwin | 76 Grand Bassam | 128 Pernambuco |
| 25 Thursday Island | 77 Sierra Leone | 129 Bahia |
| 26 Roebuck Bay (Broome) | 78 Conakry | 130 Rio de Janeiro |
| 27 Perth | 79 Bissao | 131 Santos |
| 28 Adelaide | 80 Bathurst | 132 Montevideo |
| 29 Melbourne | 81 Dakar | 133 Talcahuano |
| 30 Sydney | 82 St Louis | 134 Valparaiso |
| 31 Brisbane | 83 St Vincent | 135 Coquimbo |
| 32 Bundaberg | 84 Tenerife | 136 Antofagasta |
| 33 Norfolk Island | 85 Las Palmas | 137 Iquique |
| 34 Fiji | 86 Funchal | 138 Arica |
| 35 Neison | 87 Gibraltar | 139 Mollendo |
| 36 Cocos Island | 88 Algiers | 140 Chorillos |
| 37 Galle | 89 Malta | 141 Paita |
| 38 Madras | 90 Tripoli | 142 Santa Elena |
| 39 Bombay | 91 Crete | 143 Buenaventura |
| 40 Karachi | 92 Athens | 144 Panama |
| 41 Gwadar | 93 Corfu | 145 Colon |
| 42 Jask | 94 Trieste | 146 San Juan del Sur |
| 43 Bushire | 95 Livorno | 147 La Libertad |
| 44 Fao | 96 Civitavecchia | 148 San Jose |
| 45 Kerman | 97 Naples | 149 Salina Cruz |
| 46 Tehran | 98 Palermo | 150 Coatzacoalcos |
| 47 Odessa | 99 Nice | 151 Vera Cruz |
| 48 Constantinople | 100 Marseilles | 152 Tampico |
| 49 Cyprus | 101 Lisbon | 153 Galveston |
| 50 Port Said | 102 Vigo | 154 Esquimault/Vancouver |
| 51 Alexandria | 103 Bilbao | 155 Ascension Island |
| 52 Jedda | 104 Brest | |

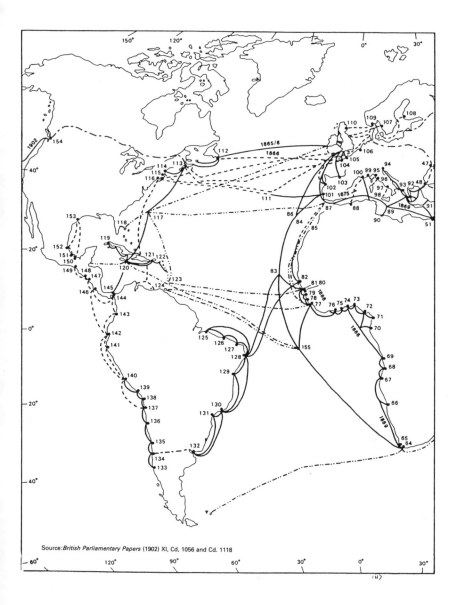

Source:*British Parliamentary Papers* (1902) XI, Cd, 1056 and Cd. 1118

**Map 10  International Communications: Telegraphs, 1865–1914**

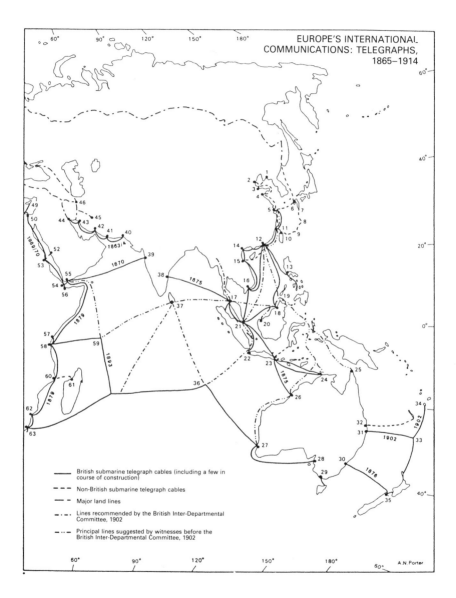

Source: Porter, *Atlas of British Overseas Expansion*, pp. 150–1.

**Table 2**
**A. Military Presence in the Dutch East Indies**

| | Land forces | | Navy | | (Auxiliary |
|---|---|---|---|---|---|
| | Total | Acheh | Total | Ships | Squadron) |
| 1870 | 27,200 | | 4,000 | 31 | (7) |
| 1873 | 29,000 | (3,400)[a] | 2,900 | 24 | (3) |
| 1874 | 29,300 | (7,500)[b] | 3,800 | 26 | (4) |
| 1875 | 29,800 | 6,300 | 3,500 | 29 | (4) |
| 1878 | 33,800 | 8,000 | | | |
| 1879 | 36,600 | 10,600 | | | |
| 1880 | 31,500 | 7,500 | 3,600 | 28 | (4) |
| 1885 | 30,400 | 5,300 | 3,800 | 28 | (4) |
| 1890 | 32,500 | 6,000 | 3,100 | 26 | (4) |
| 1895 | 34,600 | 5,800 | 3,800 | 26 | (4) |
| 1896 | 40,200 | 8,200 | | | |
| 1897 | 41,200 | 8,000 | | | |
| 1898 | 41,200 | 8,100 | | | |
| 1900 | 39,400 | 7,200 | 3,400 | 23 | (6) |
| 1905 | 36,900 | 5,700 | 3,900 | 22 | (5) |

[a] 1st expedition.
[b] 2nd expedition.
*Note*: Figures refer to the actual presence at the end of each year; in 1878, 1896 and 1898 about 10,000 troops were deployed in Acheh. Between 1870 and 1905 the share of the European element in the colonial army gradually declined from nearly 50 per cent to less than 40 per cent.
*Source*: M. Kuitenbrouwer, *The Netherlands and the Rise of Modern Imperialism: Colonies and Foreign Policy 1870–1902*, trans H. Beyer (1985; Oxford, 1991) p. 375. Reproduced by permission of Berg Publishers.

**Table 2** (*continued*)
**B. British Colonial Garrisons 1881**

| | |
|---|---|
| Canada | 1,820 |
| Bermuda | 2,200 |
| West Indies | |
|   Bahamas | 101 |
|   Jamaica | 778 |
|   Honduras | 247 |
|   Barbados | 813 |
|   Trinidad | 121 |
|   British Guiana | 246 |
| Gibraltar | 4,158 |
| Malta | 5,626 |
| Cyprus | 420 |
| Sierra Leone | 441 |
| Gold Coast | 191 |
| Cape Colony | 4,848 |
| St Helena | 210 |
| Mauritius | 355 |
| India | |
|   British troops | 69,647 |
|   Native troops | 125,000 |
| Ceylon | 1,224 |
| Hong Kong | 1,167 |
| Straits Settlements | 1,028 |

In addition to these troops, 65,809 were stationed in Britain itself and a further 25,353 in Ireland

*Source*: A. N. Porter (ed.), *Atlas of British Overseas Expansion* (London, Routledge, 1991), p. 120.

# Index

Portugal, 4, 7, 19, 21, 37, 44, 45, 60, 69, 71, 75
prestige, 18–20
Providence, 24

race, 22, 24–5
*Ralliement*, 36
raw materials, 39–41, 75
resistance, 51, 56–7, 72–3
Rhodes, Cecil John, 28
Rio de Oro, 5
Rio Muni, 5
Rivière, Henri, 70
Robinson, R.E., 51–5, 57
Rome, 1, 49
Royal Niger Company, 45
Russia, 4, 5, 15, 24, 25, 26, 37, 40, 45, 46, 50, 52, 60–1, 71, 72, 77

Said, Edward W., 65–8
St Petersburg, 49
Sakhalin, 4
Salisbury, Lord (3rd Marquess), 16, 24, 45
Samoa, 5, 74
Samori Touré, 53
Sao Tomé, 53
Schumpeter, Joseph A., 8–9
Segou, 23
Semmel, Bernard, 34–5
Senegal, 4, 53
Shantung, 5
shipping, 2, 47–8, 56, 75
Siam, 24
Sierra Leone, 4
Singapore, 4
Sino-Japanese War (1894–5), 77
slave trade, 20, 22
slavery, 20, 22, 76
social change, 24–5, 31–8
social darwinism, 24
social imperialism, 31–8, 39
Société des Mission Africaines, 53

Somaliland, 4, 5, 15
South African War (1899–1902), 62, 77
Spain, 1, 5, 60
Spanish-American War (1898), 5, 74
Spanish Sahara, 5
Sudan, Western, 4, 19, 53
Suez Canal, 52

Taiwan, *see* Formosa
Tanganyika, 5, 70
tariffs, 35, 53, 60–1, 75
technology, 2, 6, 20, 23, 25, 72, 75–7
telegraphs, 2, 112–13 (Map 10)
Tennyson, Alfred, 24
Tientsin, Treaty of (1885), 73
Timor, 4
Tirpitz, Admiral Alfred von, 32
Togo, 5
Tonkin, 73
trade, 2, 6, 7, 22, 44–9, 53–6, 59–64, 69
Tripoli, 15
Tunisia, 4, 15, 36
Turkey, 7, 45–6

United States of America (USA), 3, 5, 6, 38, 40, 50, 57, 60–1, 74

Venice, 1
Vietnam, 73

Wahabis, 56
Wales, 7
Wallerstein, Immanuel, 59–60, 62, 66
Wehler, Hans-Ulrich, 32–8
Wilhelm II, Kaiser, 19
Williams, Raymond, 66
Wolf, Eugen, 17

Yangtze, 4